Separated at Earth

Separated at Earth

Linda Jamison

and

Terry Jamison

DEDICATION

**This book is dedicated to all the heroes
who died on 9/11.**

*"We are one soul, joined at the heart,
separated at Earth."*
- Terry and Linda Jamison

CONTENTS

Separated at Earth

INTRODUCTION

Separated at Earth is the incredible, yet entirely true story of "The Psychic Twins," identical twins who overcame a lifetime of baffling, misdiagnosed illness and unspeakable pain -- from migraines to cancer -- to emerge as the premier psychic voice of this generation. Born in West Chester, Pennsylvania, to artist parents, Terry and Linda Jamison developed their artistic and spiritual sensitivities at an early age. This dynamic duo pursued a career in the visual and performing arts in New York City during the '80s, becoming noted comic performers who starred on Saturday Night Live. But chronic illness plagued them, an army of doctors gave up on them, and the twins questioned if theirs was a life worth living.

The Psychic Twins began a spiritual journey and channeled their energies into the study of metaphysics and spiritual growth. Early in life, Terry and Linda realized that they possessed a rare gift for predicting the future and contacting a broader knowing, which ultimately saved their lives. By overcoming impossible odds, they have brought a powerful message of inspiration to millions. Aside from their world prophecy, The Psychic Twins have reunited families, prevented suicides, saved marriages, and led people to the right healing tools through their intuitive counseling. Working with private detectives, they have helped to solve crimes and murder cases. This book, *Separated at Earth*, is the culmination of fifteen years of writing and rewriting. If there were any ghostwriters involved, they were real ghosts!

The Psychic Twins have become known as two of the most reputable psychics in the world, with loyal clients in over forty countries. Terry and Linda Jamison are the only psychics who publicly predicted the World Trade Center terrorist attacks (national radio show "Art Bell: Coast to Coast AM" Nov. 2,

1

1999), as well as the May 2000 stock market crash. They have appeared on fifty TV shows both in the U.S. and in England, are profiled in eleven documentary films, and have hosted three major network pilots (NBC, FOX TV, and UPN).

Featured in *The 100 Top Psychics in America* (Simon and Schuster), *The Book of Twins* (Doubleday), and *Identical*, the Jamison Twins will soon be publishing a series of psychic development books and cd's, as well as a series of their original angelic artwork. This is their first book. Read it at the risk of being enlightened, inspired, and amused.

For more information and updates, please visit their website **www.psychictwins.com**.

Chapter One

APOCALYPSE NOW

"Sweet dreams and flying machines in pieces on the ground..."

- James Taylor

We Speak

Art Bell was interviewing us, The Psychic Twins, on his live radio show "Coast to Coast AM." The date was November 2, 1999.

Twenty million listeners worldwide tune in to this nationally syndicated show that focuses on controversial and mystical subjects. If you're involved in the paranormal field, it is a great honor to be invited to guest on Art's show, as thousands of people approach his producers for such an opportunity. "Coast to Coast AM " became the fourth most popular radio show in the country during the 1990s. This particular program addressed Y2K and millennium prophecies. Art Bell interviewed us for two hours and then invited listeners to call in with their questions.

There is one call we will never forget.

Caller: *I just wanted to say I'd like the twins to generalize a little more on the upcoming events of national disasters or anything like that, I'm sort of making a list.*

Terry: *Are you talking about natural disasters, or..?*

Art: *Well, natural or unnatural. Sure.*

3

Linda: *We are seeing a lot of natural disasters in terms of earthquakes and hurricanes, blizzards coming up, especially within the next ten to twelve years. A lot of activity like that because of global warming.*
We are seeing various terrorist attacks on Federal Government... excuse me, federal buildings.
Terry: *Yes... and also the New York Trade Center. The World Trade Center. By 2002, something with a terrorist attack. Yes.[i]*

The show was broadcast live on November 2, 1999. Almost two years before the cataclysmic event of September 11, 2001 occurred.

The day before our radio show interview, we spent the entire day on November 1st preparing for our "Millennium Prophecies." Sitting side by side in our living room in West Hollywood, California, we went into a "conscious trance" state, and allowed our hands to be maneuvered across the page, used our method of automatic writing to channel information from the Akashic Records. Accessing the Akashic Records, as you will later learn more about, is like tuning into a cosmic Web library where all thoughts, deeds and actions are recorded. We asked to receive information on every topic we could think of: war, disease breakthroughs, air disasters, the stock market, politics and the topic on everyone's mind, Y2K. Through accessing the Akashic Records, sometimes sentence fragments came through, sometimes dates, names and places, almost as if we were human Ouija boards.

After about 10 minutes, Linda printed in bold capital letters:

**WORLD TRADE TOWERS TERRORIST ATTACK
BY 2002, NEW YORK CITY. ATTACKS ON
GOVERNMENT FEDERAL BUILDINGS,
WASHINGTON D.C. BIN LADEN. THOUSANDS
PERISH. PLANE CRASH, AMERICAN AIRLINES.
UNITED AIRLINES. AS MANY AS 5000 KILLED.
BOMBING.**

Linda had looked up from her writing, wide-eyed, and glanced at Terry.

Terry nodded solemnly, realizing she'd gotten the same message. Chills went up our spines. As we compared notes, we found that most of our predictions were identical. We frequently find that our written predictions match, even when we are sitting in different rooms while we work. But an event of this magnitude, in such great detail--even we were surprised.

Doing prophecy work usually does not scare us, probably because we have to be detached emotionally to allow our conscious minds to step aside so that detailed information can come in from our guides. We are literally accessing information fields from other realms. The fear comes later, after the prophecy comes true, because of the weight of responsibility of being perhaps the only ones who, for whatever reason, have been singled out to be the receivers of that knowledge. In addition, we were concerned that because of the graveness of this information, we might look like silly New Age quacks to the millions of listeners worldwide. For this reason most psychics will not make public appearances, and many use pseudonyms.

Yet our inner voices compelled us to take the risk, despite neither of us having much interest in politics or focusing on past terrorist attacks. While we were vaguely aware of the 1991 bombing in the World Trade Center, we had moved to Los

Angeles by that time, and it did not have much impact on us. With this startling news flowing through us, it felt as if we were being called to be "speakerphones" for a higher purpose, to encourage, educate and yes, warn people of what was to come.

When we thought of those two grand towers in New York, however, the monolithic symbols of American power, wealth and industry, we couldn't help but remember an earlier association with them. In the early 80's, during our days as comics and singers, we had performed at a party on the top of the World Trade Center, in Windows on the World, the huge restaurant on the top floor of one of the towers. We had jokingly dubbed ourselves "Miss Twin Towers," a name that stayed with us because we stood six-foot-two in heels.

We vividly recalled performing there on that stormy night in October 1980. We were in our dressing room putting on makeup for the show. The winds were so powerful we felt the tower swaying side to side. Hearing the whooshing sounds the gusts made around and between the two gigantic towers, Terry commented to Linda, "This is not good. This building is so fragile." Linda nodded in agreement. We had a very ominous feeling about it, but we had to get in costume and start the show.

Twenty years later, we were now envisioning the demise of the World Trade Towers within the next two years. We wondered what the consequences would be if we shared this prophecy on the Art Bell Show.

What if we were wrong?

Would we be alarming millions of people unnecessarily? If the events came to pass, would the FBI arrest us as suspects since we knew more than we should? Our guides told us that we needed to openly share what we knew. While we knew following that advice was the right thing to do, we admitted to each other our growing apprehension.

Besides the 9/11 prophecy on that particular radio show in 1999, we also predicted other events that came true. A female astrologer called in to ask what we saw around May of 2000. She had detected an unusual planetary alignment, known as a "harmonic convergence," that would occur during that time period. In answer to her question, we told her that the stock market would crash in May of 2000. Exactly as we predicted, in May of 2000 the Dow and Nasdaq did in fact experience their biggest point drop in history. Even the economists on Wall Street did not see it coming, and trillions of dollars were lost. A male caller asked us who would be our next president. We predicted the George W. Bush Presidential win. At the time, he had not yet been nominated. (We also accurately predicted the re-election of Bush in 2004). Art Bell declined to hazard a guess about who the next president would be. We predicted a shooting in Seattle, which actually happened six hours after our show aired.

The clock flashed 2:00 a.m. when we ended the show. We were exhausted but wired. We were shocked to have made so many predictions of such huge impact to 20 million listeners worldwide. What would come of all this?

The next morning we heard the news: There had been a shooting in Seattle--five people shot--just as we had predicted six hours earlier. Our friend from Seattle, Shavawn, called us to report the news; she had listened to our millennium predictions the night before. We felt uneasy. What else would happen?

Eight hundred people called us during the week following that radio appearance, most of whom booked readings with us. Some of the callers have since become our most regular clients, and many have become friends. But we were unprepared for the volume of calls. This was the biggest appearance to date. We had to hire a girlfriend to return calls and help us to book the readings. We became so busy we did not have much time to ponder which of our other predictions would come to pass.

But during the weeks just prior to Sept. 11, 2001, both of us had the heaviest sense of foreboding, a gut feeling that something huge was about to happen that would forever alter the path of our lives. Still, even our psychic gifts could not prepare us for the magnitude of the events that would transpire. We will never forget the eerie, disquieting feeling we had on the morning of September 11, 2001.

The phone rang early. Too early. Terry dragged herself out of bed. It was our friend Susan. "Turn on the news!" Susan screamed. "The World Trade Center is on fire!"

We watched as the first tower went down in the billowing smoke. Terry replied, "Susan, we predicted this on the radio, back in 1999."

"They said on TV that they think it was an accident," Susan replied. Linda had picked up the extension phone. "It's no accident, it's Bin Laden," she said. "It's terrorism."

Susan gasped in disbelief. The second tower fell minutes later. Tears streamed down our faces and we watched in horror as our prophecy came true. We learned later that we were the only psychics who had publicly predicted the biggest terrorist attack in history. The proof is on tape.

We felt a complex mixture of every kind of emotion, ranging from grief and rage to absolute horror. On one level we were completely distraught, not only by the horrifying spectacle we were witnessing along with the rest of the world, but by the shock of seeing our most earth-shaking prediction come true. We also felt great pain on a personal level, because of our connection with the towers and the people of New York. Were any of our friends in those buildings? Were our friends in New York going to be safe?

In the ensuing days, word of our prophecy spread over the Internet. A producer from Larry King Live flew in from Atlanta to interview us. Strangers were calling in--they had saved our phone number from the Art Bell Show interview--exclaiming that they had heard us on the show, and remembered what we had said about the New York World Trade Center attack. Some people called to inform us that the FBI had shut down their websites because our predictions were posted on them.

Horrified, we ran to our computer and punched in our website domain name: www.psychictwins.com. "ACCESS DENIED" flashed up on the screen. Our site had been shut down. We felt numb with fear. We believe it was the FBI. Would we be investigated? Was our phone being tapped? How far would they go? All kinds of crazy thoughts raced through our heads. It wasn't like there was anybody we could call for advice.

Who in the world ever had this kind of experience?

That same week, astrologer Terry Guardino invited us on his astrology TV show to talk about our predictions. During the taping of that show, we predicted the date that the United States would declare war on Afghanistan: Oct. 7, 2001. On that very day, our military launched its first strikes on Afghanistan in Kabul, Kandahar, and Jalalabad.

In the weeks following the events of 9/11, many people questioned us about the prophecy. How in the world did you know? How does your information come through? Do you always write your predictions? Did you both write identical information? How did you feel when it actually happened?

Most frequently we heard people ask, what else is coming?

We felt a responsibility to inform the public about coming events, and more importantly, to comfort people and put them at ease. So many were in utter terror, insane with panic. Some of our friends living in New York had lost many loved ones in the

Towers and were completely devastated. They called us in hysterics, and we spent hours consoling them. The event had caused unimaginable suffering all across the country, and we were picking up the pieces, helping them to get a sense of power and control back in their lives. Many were consumed with thoughts of revenge, others by fear of another possible attack. Counseling others was the one powerful way that we could get through our own grief, and it kept us grounded in the midst of all the chaos.

We spent the next days and weeks channeling higher communication on future events-- from bio-weapons to the war in Afghanistan. Friends in Los Angeles were buying gas masks for their young children and stocking up on supplies. They asked us, would the water supply be poisoned? Would their children be safe? Would their relatives be safe if they flew anywhere? Could the country be obliterated? How many terror cells were there? No one felt safe. Airline attendants called us to find out if their jobs were secure. Thousands of airline workers were laid off. We had made the prediction that United Airlines would go bankrupt in the final months of 2002, which ultimately did happen.

We were as enraged as the clients and loved ones we counseled. Why had the government missed this blatant attack? The best agents in U.S. intelligence did not respond, despite warnings, signs, predictions. We felt that thousands of people had died because our government had ignored warnings and failed to protect them.

As spiritual teachers, we tried to get people to look at the tragic events from a larger perspective, which seemed almost impossible in the wake of such devastation. We wanted to help them find in this tragedy an opportunity for healing and human awakening. In subsequent months, we noticed that the incident had altered the way Americans felt about themselves, their country and their relationship with the rest of the world. Ram Dass, the spiritual teacher, once said that suffering forces confrontation. The people of the world, especially in America, now needed to face their darkest fears, their deepest negativity, on a profound level. As horrific as this event was, it served as a profound karmic lesson we could not have learned any other way.

We feel everyone can benefit from the self-reflection frightening events provoke. However, we still feel compelled to share our predictions, even if only as warnings of potential destruction. It is our belief these prophetic disclosures from an unseen plane come through us so that we can potentially help people avoid more pain and suffering.

As human beings, we are awakening from a long, deep sleep. September 11 was an opportunity to respond nonviolently to raise the consciousness and healing of our planet. We believe it was to teach us to make choices out of love and compassion rather than from a place of judgment, blame, control, and revenge.

The ancient civilization of Atlantis was considered to be something of an Eden on Earth, according to Plato. The Atlanteans became decadent and arrogant, which led to their ultimate destruction. Cataclysms of earthquakes, tidal waves and volcanoes rocked the once Utopian society. We are facing similar events, in light of the tsunami in 2004, which has destroyed the lives of so many people. (Linda had recurring nightmares about the tsunami for years leading up to it). In Buddhism, there is a principle called esho funi, which means the oneness of man and his environment. It means that our outer world reflects our innermost feelings and emotions. Native American Indians believe this too, that respecting each other and the planet will reflect in a healthy Earth, and peace among its peoples. A life out of balance will create a planet out of balance. The essence of Gandhi's teachings was fearlessness. In the midst of enormous adversity, he faced everyone, including his enemies, with courage and love. We hope that 9/11 allows us all to rediscover our humanity and to choose love instead of fear.

We feel our work as psychics and artists serves to help people along that higher path. Sometimes just the right encouraging words or an insightful missing piece of information about themselves or others is all someone needs to bring understanding, peace and renewal to their lives.

One might think that having psychic gifts has made our own lives easy. While we enjoy a deeply spiritual richness of heart, we have still encountered great obstacles and problems in every area of our lives. In that way, we are no different than you are, dear reader. But we do feel that in the process of facing our severe adversities while never giving up on our dreams, we discovered our true calling to be an open channel of healing for others. In the following chapters, we will share with you our story: from the mundane to the bizarre, from the heights of happiness to the depths of almost-fatal illness. We will also reveal how we have come to be known as "The Psychic Twins" and what it is like to live a life with heightened sight.

---

[1] Excerpt from transcript of taped "Coast to Coast AM" show, November 2, 1999.

- *As a side note, there were many symbolic double numbers around 9/11: Flight 11 crashed into the Twin Towers on "Two's-Day" the 11th. Flight 77, which crashed into the Pentagon, is also a double number.*

Chapter Two

SMALL MEDIUMS AT LARGE

We are so excited! We're at the East Bradford Elementary School fair, we are six years old, and we can't believe all the fun activities that have transformed our modest school playground. We take turns throwing ping-pong balls into tiny glass fishbowls, and lo and behold, Linda has won a bright orange goldfish! Our first pet! She is clutching the baggie full of water and fish when we approach the gypsy fortune-teller booth. Sitting on the table in front of the smiling, toothless gypsy is a large glass jar filled to the brim with jellybeans.

"Guess how many beans are in the jar and win what's in the secret chest!" the gypsy says in a low, smoker's voice. Without hesitation, Terry chimes "537!" It turns out that is the exact number (but she knew that!) The gypsy gives Terry a little key, she opens the treasure chest, and there is her prize, a bright rainbow-colored beach ball. A good guess? We think not. This is the earliest "psychic" experience that we can remember.

Our life began as an egg that split.

We made our earthly debut back when Marilyn was the feminine ideal, Elvis was already fat, Rock Hudson appeared straight, politicians were still on good terms with the press, and the nation was in a perpetual state of naïveté. Women's lib was still unheard of, Vietnam and Watergate hadn't happened yet. Television was new and PCs and the Internet had not yet been invented.

In our little Philadelphia suburb of West Chester, people left their front doors unlocked and children played in fresh air and talked politely to strangers. Little twin girls took dance and piano lessons, created art projects from scraps of felt, construction paper, and glue, sewed their own dresses and dreamed of having a marriage like Donna Reed.

The wildness of the sixties seemed like a bad psychedelic trip someone else was having in a distant universe. We were so sheltered in our small country town, and the reverberations of drugs, free love, war and civic unrest were surreal and frightening to us. The Kennedy and King assassinations, political protests and the drug and sexual revolution swirled past us like a dream, bearing no apparent relevance to us or our future. Our family and our neighbors lived insular lives quite unaffected by the ugly realities of society at large. There existed a disquieting sense of denial, as if a tacit agreement had been made never to admit that people suffered, that there were in fact dark energies at work in our world, in our town, even in our home.

It was in this oppressive climate of fear and naiveté that the two of us were raised. As precocious children, we longed to heal the disparity between the vastly different worlds of heaven and hell, heaven being the forced gaiety, the "fool's paradise" that was the Zeitgeist of our childhood years, and hell being the pulsing, imminent cataclysm that lurked around every corner of our intuition.

Years after our birth, our mother told us that she knew she was going to have either twins... or an elephant. We were two weeks late, due on New Year's Day. Labor had to be induced on January 12th. Terry came out first, screaming, while Linda took a half-hour break, relishing her time alone in the womb. It was as if she sensed the nightmare that lay ahead, and needed the brief respite. Each twin weighed in at a nearly seven pounds, an even fourteen together. Terry Jane was named after Dad's best friend Earl Terry, who was killed in World War II, and Mom's first name "Jane." Linda's middle name was simply "B" because our parents couldn't think of a name, and so she was "Baby B". Thank God we didn't have rhyming names like "Rhonda and Yolanda," or "Fallopia and Myopia."

Three-year-old brother Flip took one look at the matching sister-set and said, "Okay, Mom, you can take them back now."

Our mother kept us side by side in a twin crib, where we would sleep holding each other. Dad Philip, or "Jamie" to his friends, once forgot which twin he fed and gave Linda both bottles while Terry cried loudly. Linda then began to cry because she was too full. Dad and Mom loved the Big Band Music of the '40s, and played it almost constantly on the radio or Victrola. When we were toddlers, at bedtime Dad used to hold us in his lap in a rocking chair and sing to us a little off key. He sang popular current hits, such as "Chattanooga Choo Choo," "That Old Black Magic," and "I'm Gonna Buy a Paper Doll."

We find it funny that the three of us kids grew up to become singers, because oddly enough, neither of our parents could carry a tune. We didn't care; their singing made us happy.

"I'd rather have a paper doll to call my own,
Than have a fickle-minded real live girl."

Just a harmless song, or was it?

Popular song lyrics of the time sent a not-so-subtle message that women were somehow inferior to men, and that their place was either in a domestic role, or as objects to be manipulated. That women were "crazy" or "ditsy" or "fickle." Years later we became "living dolls" professionally, impersonating robotized store mannequins and Barbie Dolls in our comedy act, as a way of satirizing society's view of women.

Linda and I could sing anything in perfect harmony, and we

often sang for our family at home. Dad would always comment appreciatively, "You girls should have an act."
His words were prophetic, because years later we would become professional singers. Show business was in our blood from an early age.

Everyone sarcastically called us "The Happiness Twins," because we looked anything but happy. We rarely smiled and we greeted goochy-gooers with a solemn gaze. Mom dressed us alike and it became a habit which we carried through to adulthood. Sometimes our tops or dresses were the exact same style, but in different colors. One of our favorite memories is coming home to find new school clothes laid out on our parents' double bed, identical outfits displayed side by side: matching blackwatch plaid kilts (our family is half Scottish and that is the Jamison clan plaid), preppie striped T-shirts, starchy white cotton blouses with Peter Pan collars.

People are wiser now. They dress their twins differently, keep them in separate classes, encourage separate friendships. This was not done in the '50s and '60s. Known collectively as "The Twins" to relatives and classmates, we were never able to develop confidence as unique, independently functioning human beings. At home, we both answered to the generic name "Sissy" because our family wanted to avoid the unpleasant task of making a distinction between the two of us or avoid possibly mistaking one of us for the other.

This did not strike us as odd or devaluing at the time; our little pet name seemed quite natural in view of the fact that we were exactly alike in looks, speech, clothing and manner. We consulted each other every morning on the matching outfit that was to be worn to school. We played with the same friends at the same time, received identical presents at Christmas, played with identical dolls, fought with the same annoying brother, graduated with the same grade point averages. Until we both had LASIK surgery as adults to correct our nearsightedness, we could even wear each other's contact lenses in a pinch. To everyone we were "cute" and exactly the same.

Our actions, accomplishments and feelings were lumped together by everyone, parents and teachers alike, largely due to the fact that we were perceived as a collective blob. "You twins are so talented." "The twins did it."

"One of the twins said that." Looking back, we honestly can't remember who did what. It's as if we were the same person with two bodies. Gradually, we realized we were one soul, separated at Earth.

Our humorous bones were strengthened by an eclectic assemblage of influences, most notably our mother, Jane. Born Jane Bethel Gray in 1925, Jane was the second of two daughters born to Jerome Bethel Gray, a successful advertising executive, and his wife, Miriam Fertig Gray, a registered nurse. Ours was a small and eccentric family of artists, eight blood relations in all, with no uncles, and no first or second cousins. We are descendants of Benjamin Franklin, according to our grandmother Daisy, who researched our Jamison family tree. Legend has it that all of Franklin's children were illegitimate.

Our mother had a histrionic nature and needed us to be her audience. We often felt as if she really wanted to be on the stage. She delivered lines as though she were playing to a crowded theater. We learned to react in a certain way— laughing loudly at all her jokes, which pleased her immensely. We were a great audience. She used very colorful language that would make a sailor blush, while our father would say "dagnabbit!" instead of "damn!" Mom had flaming red curly hair and a temper to match. Both she and her sister Alice were famous for their razor wit and Phyllis Diller-esque cackles. Mom's steely brown eyes flashed with the intensity of lasers. She had her ways of escaping. Every day in the summer, she would lie outside the kitchen on her plastic chaise in the sun, hoping her freckles would melt together to make an even tan. Her good friend Nancy had a deep mahogany tan and a beauty-shop hairstyle, like a magazine ad.

Mom smelled like Coppertone and Chanel No. 5.

Besides golf, our mom loved shopping, and she'd often take the two of us to Mosteller's Department store in our town, or John Wanamaker in Wilmington, and we'd stop on the way to get lengths of fabric at the fabric outlet. We loved these trips, and savored the time we spent with mom when we all had fun and she didn't feel pressured to do housework. We especially enjoyed going down the many aisles of colorful bolts of fabric, calicos and gingham checks and soft, thick wool tartans.

Our passion for designing and making clothes started early, and Linda was especially good at it. Our grandmother Daisy taught us how to sew and embroider elaborate flowers when we were eight years old, and we made many of our own clothes for school.

While making our lunch for school, Mom would tell us about her own childhood, which was a combination of privilege and abuse. That tends to explain why she had trouble letting people get too close to her, including us. She talked about growing up in their big colonial mansion, The Dower House, how she always had a matching purses and shoes for all her outfits, and we thought that was neat. Her family's maid was a stout, black woman named Elizabeth, but they all called her "Izzybuff" because that is how our mom pronounced it when she was little. Izzybuff would pack their school lunches with caviar sandwiches and petit-four desserts, and "material napkins."

Each morning Mom would hand us our little metal red plaid lunchboxes carefully packed with fluffernutter (peanut butter and marshmallow fluff) sandwiches, packaged cheese and crackers, Chocolate Tandy Takes or Mallomars and an apple, and we would head off to the bus stop, our heads filled with images of Mom and Auntie Alice living like preppie private-school girls, like characters out of "The Philadelphia Story." We couldn't afford caviar!

We loved having Mom comb our blonde hair into pigtails for school. Dad called them "paintbrushes" because they looked like the thick sable watercolor brushes he painted with. When we were six or seven, Mom would sit on the big overstuffed armchair and we'd take turns sitting between her knees while she combed our hair, meticulously parting it and putting it into two high pigtails with rubber bands. She wore her soft Lanz nightie and a warm robe, and smelled like coffee. In a little white cardboard box were lengths of brightly colored satin ribbons, and we would pick the color that went with our outfit that day. It became a daily ritual, for a while, and we savored the attention we were getting from Mom.

Our mother was good with things that involved ritual, but she absolutely hated cooking and doing housework, and frequently said so. The only household duty Mom liked was ironing. She could spend hours and hours ironing sheets, and Dad's dress shirts, almost as if it were a meditation for her. It was her chance to be alone and relax, focusing on sprinkling the clothes with water, smoothing the wrinkles with her hand and following with the little metal iron, making everything look smooth and just perfect. For just a short time, she could be peaceful and happy in her ironing room world, a world that she could control.

Grandfather Gray was an obdurate, explosive man, with orange-red hair and given to ruling with an iron fist. His keen wit and fearsome temper were the two sides of a sword's blade. Like most daughters of affluent families, Jane and her older sister Alice were not instructed in the domestic arts. The humor-as-survival mechanism became the raison d'etre in our family as well, a sort of tradition handed down through the lineage. It was like a religion. Wit was a dominant gene, the key to happiness and success. Straight A's, spirituality, compassion and other virtues were not emphasized. If you laughed at our mother's jokes, you were in. Trying to survive in the Jamison house without personality was tantamount to entering a lion's cage without a chair. It was one's sword, one's honor, and one's only and best defense. The members of the Jamison family were nothing if not stylists of humor.

We can't remember a single moment during our childhood that we weren't together, the two of us. As children, we never fought with each other. Our home was a small 200-year-old stone farmhouse in West Chester, an historic college town. Dad had purchased it for $5,000 in the early'50s. Even though it was always cold and damp, we loved that old barn of a house, with its brick kitchen floor, a Dutch oven, and musty-smelling attic. Dad once chased a bat around the attic with a tennis racket. During a spring thaw, the kitchen flooded and we had to bail out with buckets, wearing rubber galoshes. When it snowed a lot, the snow would be deeper than we were tall. Mom would zip us into our puffy snowsuits and mittens so we could run out to build a snow fort, while Dad shoveled the walk and scraped ice off of the car. When the ice covered every branch of every tree, the whole town was transformed to a magical icy wonderland and there was no sight more beautiful.

At three, we would wait patiently for the Wonder Bread man to arrive in his white truck. We would greet him excitedly at the door of the front porch and as soon as we could, we opened the plastic bag and each pulled out a piece of soft puffy white bread. Kneeling on the carpet in front of our little wooden chairs, we broke up the cottony bread into dozens of little pieces and arranged the pieces in a decorative mosaic pattern around our china plates so it would seem like more. This became a strange daily ritual for us. Sometimes we did the same thing with slices of Kraft American cheese.

As children, we developed our own secret language. This phenomenon actually has a name, it is called "idioglassia" or "cryptophasia". This is a common occurrence with twins, but it is usually outgrown in adolescence. Not so for us. Our private language, an intimate vocabulary of "mime-speak" comprised of beeps, funny words with quirky inflections and a complex system of mime-like gestures, grew even more sophisticated as we got older. We could communicate the subtlest of emotions with the software of our faces, never requiring a spoken word. But we loved language, and quite instinctively modeled a uniquely personal and witty phraseology that bemused and befuddled outsiders. Most kids go through a phase where they don't fit in with groups. It never occurred to us to try to fit in.

Why bother? We were our own club.

At night when we got into our twin beds, we would reach out and touch the tips of our forefingers together, as a sort of symbol of our spiritual oneness.

We played together, sitting for hours cross-legged in front of a chalkboard, making detailed drawings of the interiors of spaceships, of all things. At age four and five, we would use white chalk to draw the controls in painstaking detail, covering every inch of chalkboard. Was it from memory? There was always a little seat for the captain of the craft, which was usually a stuffed toy hamster. Most days we would sit side by side at our little crafts table, happily drawing, cutting, sewing, pasting.

Creativity was effortless for us.

Every year we made by hand all of Mom and Dad's Christmas cards so they could send them to their friends. Linda dreamed of one day being a fashion designer or creating fashion

illustrations like the ones in the magazines. Terry wanted to be a
Disney cartoonist when she grew up. We were artistically gifted
children, yet no one made a fuss, because our parents believed
that praise would spoil us. We had inherited our parents' talents
for drawing and painting. Dad always said we were better than
either of them. As little girls, we created elaborate drawings on
the Etch-a-Sketch, and we could draw anything easily. We
started first grade at the age of five, skipping kindergarten
because in those days you had to pay for it and our parents
couldn't afford it. We could do realistic full-figure pencil
portraits of our friends and family when we started school.

At the time, TV was relatively new. We spent long hours in
front of a boxy black-and-white Magnavox, our window to
another world. We adored *Bewitched Get Smart, The Outer
Limits, The Twilight Zone,* and *Laugh In.* Carol Burnett and
Lucy were huge influences in our becoming comics as adults.
We loved *The Patty Duke Show*, because Patty and her cousin
Kathy were identical, but they had totally different
personalities. "They laugh alike, they walk alike, at times they
even talk alike--you could lose your mind!" went the theme
song. Dick Van Dyke was also a big comedic influence on us.
But we also loved the commercials for Noxzema skin cream,
Prell shampoo, Pepsodent toothpaste and Lestoil. "It's so easy
when you use Lestoil!" or "If I only have one life, let me live it
as a blonde!" We knew all of the slogans and jingles by heart.
TV trained us early to be Pop culture junkies.

Mom always loved films, and she knew all the film stars by
name. "Oh, that's Carole Lombard!" she would say, with an
almost worshiping tone. She had seen all of the old classics
growing up. Mom was so animated, like Lucy. She could have
been a comedic actress if she had more confidence. In those
days, most women married and raised kids, and Mom seemed to
yearn for something more. She would cry out, "I'm nothing but

a maid in this house!" to which our father would reply, with a sly grin, "Don't be silly. If you were my maid, I'd have fired you *years* ago." This would make her fume.

Dad's mother, Daisy, was a soft-spoken entrepreneurial woman who opened her own restaurant during the great depression. "The High Street Coffee House" became very popular with college professors and the local businessmen and women of West Chester. After thirteen years of running the coffee shop, Daisy turned it into an antique store called The House of Jamison, which sold American furniture. Back in the forties, Daisy had written and published a small book about making lampshades. For a number of years when they were first married, Dad and Mom had a small business designing and making custom-made lampshades that were very special. Our parents were actually commissioned to illustrate people's homes in pen and ink and watercolor on the shades, and punched holes in the little windowpanes so it looked like lights were on inside. We thought they were beautiful and very clever.

In 1958 our parents gave up the lampshade business to devote their energy exclusively to painting. Both our parents were master watercolorists and Dad would become nationally renowned for his beautiful landscapes and flower paintings in the Brandywine River School tradition, also known as "The Wyeth School." Noted painter Andrew Wyeth lived a stone's throw away from us in neighboring Chadds Ford, and his style was a strong influence on Dad's work. He used the same muted color palette of rich olive greens, deep blue-grays, warm siennas and yellow ochres. So did Mom, who adapted her style to complement our father's. As a painter, our mother always said she felt like she was in his shadow, and lacked the confidence and drive our father had. Dad's paintings were like visual symphonies. The walls of our house were covered with watercolors and oil paintings, painted by our parents as well as other artists. Our father is retired now, but he likes to frequent local art auctions.

Some of our mother's friends didn't understand that while their husbands went to work in an office wearing a suit and tie every day, our dad didn't. He went to "The Studio," which was in our grandmother Daisy's house at 303 South High Street, and he'd paint pictures for eight hours and come home. He worked very hard but painting was always a true passion for him, and he had the discipline and vision of a real master. It is difficult for some people to grasp that painting isn't simply playing around, but a job that requires tremendous talent, focus and concentration (a lot like psychic work). Dad sold out his first exhibition. He was only 25. His career gradually built from there, and he won many awards for his work.

One day our Dad was commissioned by NASA to illustrate the Apollo-Soyuz space shuttle launch. He got to wear a white space suit and everybody thought he was an astronaut. These paintings now hang in the National Air and Space Museum in Washington, D.C. They depict a beautiful landscape of flowers with a high-tech rocket ship taking off in the distance, a comment on the juxtaposition of traditional nature and modern technology.

Chapter Three

YA-YA SISTERHOOD

*"What greater thing is there for two human souls to feel that
they are joined, to strengthen each other, in silent unspeakable
memories."*

- George Eliot

We remember Dad's back. We don't remember our father in
those days so much as we remember his back. Watching the
back of his head while driving on those long summer road trips
to Maine, never stopping because he wanted to drive straight
through. Watching his back in the studio, in his black sweatshirt
hunching over a painting, smoking or watching TV. He was
physically present, more than his own father had been.
Everyone wishes his or her father would play with them more,
interact, talk with them, discuss things. Few fathers knew how
to connect with little girls back then. Most are not so good at it
now, either. He was there but not there. It seemed like his mind
was a million miles away, thinking about his paintings. He used
to put a quarter on the dinner table and promise that whoever
didn't speak during dinner would get paid with it. We would
stifle our giggles, and the desperate desire to share, but the tacit
message was "children should be seen and not heard." We often
left the dinner table with severe stomach pains.

Our family was far from wealthy, but we were comfortable
and lived a simple life. The furniture in our house was mostly
Shaker style, with hard straight chairs and benches made of
polished walnut in clean lines, very austere. It was sort of like
living in a monastery, except for the little touches of color in the
paintings on the wall, or a shock of orange and red pillows on

the slate gray couch. Selectivity of color use was important.
Dad and Mom were proud of their "Taste."

Dad disdained "gaudiness," or garish use of color and pattern
and often said so. He preferred neutral earthy tones. He learned
very late in life that he was slightly color-blind, and after
cataract surgery he started painting with much brighter colors.

Because we lived on a busy street, we were not allowed to
have pets, but there were plenty of stuffed dead animals in the
attic. Our great-grandfather, David McCadden, was the inventor
of modern taxidermy, or the archival mounting of animals in
lifelike form. A hunter, he worked at the Academy of Natural
Sciences for fifty years. There were musty-smelling stuffed
owls and squirrels and raccoons in our house, a lion's head, and
a collection of American Indian relics in a glass case
downstairs: arrowheads, tomahawks and knives. Small wonder
we would one day feel so comfortable communicating with the
dead! Our house was full of creepy spirit energies.

We idolized our father. He was extremely well-liked, a quiet
and honest man who did not interact with us much. His world
was that of painting, and we felt very separate. He drank Black
Label beer, and for years he chain-smoked Pall Malls. We used
to plead that our parents not leave home so much for their
cocktail parties.

Our brother, older by a few years, was a mystery to us all. He
was a loner. Flippy was thin and lanky, with dark, intense eyes.
Dad called him "Flipper McDipper." He hated shopping for
clothes, and always wore mismatching shirts and pants because
he didn't care a whit about style. This was absolutely
incomprehensible to us. Mom would constantly badger him
about his clothes, and try to get him to wear complementary
things, but he wouldn't pay any attention. At Christmas, he
would receive a sweater and new shirts, and they were quickly
tossed aside with a grimace.

Flip was always brilliantly funny, like a cross between Groucho Marx and Woody Allen. We would strain to listen to Flip's sarcastic remarks because he would speak them very quietly, as if to himself, and they were always hilarious. He was, as it turned out, our polar opposite in terms of his personality and interests. What we shared was his dry, sardonic humor and an appreciation for the absurd. We didn't communicate much, and he kept to himself, absorbed in his private single-person world.

One Saturday we came home to find that our standard piano had been replaced with an upright player piano in our living room. Our brother bought it with his own money. We have vivid memories of the family singing around Flip's player piano. As the bellows sucked air through the paper holes of the music roll, we would belt out old Presidential campaign tunes from the turn of the century in three-part harmony. The lyrics were printed on the roll.

"I like Ike, and Ike is easy to like!" was a family favorite. "Tippecanoe and Tyler too!" "Get on the raft with Taft boys, get in the winning boat!" Flip would sometimes hook a fake curly beard over his ears and belt out Gilbert and Sullivan operas in a hearty baritone, while brandishing a sword, alone in the living room downstairs. Years later, when he was in his thirties, he starred in local Gilbert and Sullivan operas that were put on by the local State College.

When Flippy graduated from high school, our parents were horrified when he eschewed Wharton business school and instead left home to study with a blind man at the Jim Simms School of Piano Tuning in Georgia. Like the two of us, Flippy always marched to his own drummer. A stringed instrument expert now, he lives with his lovely lady friend Lucille in an historic house in West Chester. It is filled with vintage pianos, harpsichords, cafe organs, nickelodeons and antique music boxes that he rebuilds and sells all over the world.

Linda speaks

As kids, Terry and I used to obsess over games. It was as if we were being guided at an early age to master intensely focused activities. Every moment we had to be challenging ourselves in some way to improve our mental or physical skills. We had a Magic 8 Ball that we would consult about the future for hours on end. Important questions, really important ones, like did Joey McNeill like Terry and would we make the cheerleading squad? In fact, we used it so much that we broke it, and the little triangle that floated to the surface of the liquid would say only "Ask Again Later." This was infuriating! We needed answers!! (P.S. We never made the cheerleading squad, probably due in part to the fact that we were total nerds).

As little girls of about eight years old, we became fascinated with a clever game called "The Labyrinth." It was just a small wooden box, the top of which was a wooden board that could tilt in various directions with the use of little knobs on each side. On the tilting board were many intersecting wooden pieces that formed a maze. The object of the game was to maneuver a little metal ball around the maze, while avoiding the several dozen holes where the ball could fall in. We practiced this game for hours and hours at a time, finally both mastering it to the point where almost every time we could get from beginning to end in about three minutes without ever once losing the ball. This game trained our focus and revealed our tendency toward obsessive compulsive behaviors. It also would come to be somewhat of a metaphor for our life struggle, which is very like a labyrinth, a maze where we have been challenged to negotiate one trial after another.

We spent every summer on a little island called Vinalhaven

off the southern coast of Maine. Our summer home there was on Pleasant Street. Across from our house lived the Reverend Peacock and his wife and son, Phillip, a playmate of ours. Down the street lived our parents' good friends Ducky and Ruthie, and their four kids. Ducky Haskell was a local lobsterman and council member. He was a stocky man with a big walrus moustache, smoked a pipe, and had very kind eyes that were always smiling, as if he knew a secret.

Our grandmother Daisy had bought an inn on the island called "Bridgeside" which overlooked the ocean. It was a big, rambling place and we would spend hours keeping a lot of little old ladies company.

Barbara Morton's antique shop was right behind our house. We remember at age five riding in the Fourth of July parade on her big wooden antique wagon, with old pots and pans clanging, the two of us dressed in taffy-striped dresses and starchy white aprons, holding a sign that read "NO TWO ALIKE."

"Ain't they cunnin'!" the islanders would exclaim, which meant we were cute. Mom would get many admiring comments as she pushed us around town in our double stroller. No one on the island had ever seen twins before. We were like a strange omen.

Sometimes mom took us swimming "down the quarry," as the islanders would say. Tall sheer cliffs surrounded an old granite quarry, and it was so majestic there, so beautiful. We loved the pine trees and the solitude of this secret place. The smell of pine and the cold clear water. Vinalhaven Island had been a major source of granite in the country for buildings on the East Coast. It felt so private and pure there, and we felt free.

We would help Mom hang out the wash on the line. Crisp white sheets snapped in the breeze, against a hard blue sky, catching the island sun like giant sails. "Good dryer day, Jane!" our neighbor Burt Dyer, the lobsterman, would shout to our mother, and she would smile and wave. We could hear Paul Harvey's distinctive radio voice coming from Dad's studio in the back room of the house. Dad had a big old 1940's wooden radio that was only tuned to Paul Harvey, and a station that played Top 40 songs. Dad was working on some paintings of Smith's Point from some photographs he had taken. The room smelled of glue and paint. His big work table was covered with large vases and shiny cream-colored ceramic pitchers filled with island wildflowers in hues of yellow and orange. Watercolor sketches and drawings of daisies in fields were tacked up on the wall, and a weathered American flag leaned against a window. He liked to put that flag in a lot of his paintings. His paintings of interiors always had a lonely, wistful quality about them, as if someone had just left the room and would not return.

On days that Dad's friend Burt was drunk, he would stagger across our lawn, his galoshes unbuttoned and flapping, calling for our father. He smelled like a brewery. Mom would hurry us upstairs and we'd hide in one of the closets until he was gone. Sometimes Dad brewed him a cup of strong, black coffee to "sober him up," then sent him home to his wife Gladys, a large, dark Indian woman with wild black hair and flashing eyes. She scared us too.

We were "summer jerks," but we were popular with the island folks. Vinalhaven was idyllic in some ways, but it was actually quite repressed. Young people had little to entertain them, and the island was very isolated from the mainland, which was an hour and a half away by ferry. Many of the girls got pregnant as teenagers. By the time they were twenty they had two or three kids. There were mysterious fires. The bowling alley and the only movie theatre burned down, and there was talk it was for insurance money. If the islanders didn't like you, make no mistake--they would saw your boat in half. The two of us used to call Vinalhaven "The Crucible."

There was a hotel at the Jersey shore called "The Nautilus." It was owned by our parents' friends. We would all go down to Stone Harbor, New Jersey, for a few days in the stifling heat of August. The Nautilus was right on the beach, suspended like a pier, on a foundation of huge logs that sunk vertically into the sand. We remember loving the beach and spent hours jumping the waves, hand in hand. One summer we made a sea serpent out of sand. Like a huge boa constrictor, it started at the ocean's edge and curved a hundred yards up the beach almost to the street. As the tide crept in, we squealed with delight as our serpent dissolved. A few years later, The Nautilus was destroyed by a tidal wave and washed out to sea. Years later, Terry did many paintings of sea serpents, one of them titled "Fun at the Beach."

Our teachers were terrible, dry and unimaginative. We had to make our own inspiration through our art and humor. In spite of our teachers' shortcomings, we survived and managed straight A's. We actually loved studying and learning, and rarely missed school. The two of us especially loved English and writing, and excelled at it. We were much younger and smaller than the other students, and we had some concentration problems—it was very difficult for us to focus. So we had to work harder to excel.

But we firmly believed that if we were perfect, we would be loved.

We were precocious readers. As young children we loved to read The Nancy Drew adventures and mysteries by Agatha Christie. In our early teens we read books like *The Female Eunuch* by Germaine Greer, *The Greening of America* by Charles Reich, and *Lolita* by Vladimir Nabakov. Linda never missed a program called *Discovery,* all about what the world would be like in the year 2000, and she would take copious notes. She was fascinated by the future and its possible inventions. When the new millennium finally came around, we were both disappointed that everyone wasn't wearing disposable silver spacesuits or using the futuristic products the program had described. Our imaginations had always been way ahead of our time, and it seemed as if things were moving at the speed of mud.

One full moon night, our Dad's father, Philip Jamison, Sr., showed up at our door. We had never seen him before, and hadn't heard much about him. We remember only that he was an alcoholic, that Dad's mother Daisy had left him and taken Dad with her when he was four years old. Rumor had it he subsequently lost all his money in bad real estate investments. The night he came to visit, he brought us little musical jewelry boxes with ballerinas that twirled magically to the tune "Fur Elise" in front of a mirror. Inside were tiny pink pearl necklaces. We never saw him again.

Chapter Four

DANCING WITH MYSELF

"Send in the clones."

We Speak

Almost everyone seems to have a fascination with twins. People have always stopped us to say, "Oh, you are so lucky! I always wanted to be a twin." Trust us, we know how lucky we are, but we didn't always feel that way.

In fact, we had a power struggle with each other for many years. We are closer now than any twins you'll ever meet, but that is a result of a lifetime of working on our relationship. It is very much like a marriage, and at times it seemed like a bad marriage. As adults, we entered therapy together to learn how to communicate more effectively with each other. Most twins have confided in us that they could never live together because of the volatility of their relationship. Some twins even choose to live on opposite coasts! The power struggle can be extreme, and at times overwhelming.

There is no denying that a unique bond exists between twins. We are identical, or monozygotic, which means the egg splits in half, and becomes two people who are genetically 100 per cent the same person. The same person. The only real clones. So you can imagine how close a bond we have. Nowadays with the broad use of fertility drugs, many twins are being born, but these twins are seldom identical, they are "fraternal." This means two different eggs, two different people genetically, that are fertilized by two different sperm. Fraternal twins often look very different from one another, whereas identical twins look, well-- identical!

A lot of people greeted us with the slogan, "Which twin has the Toni?" because it was a popular home perm commercial in the sixties. Another popular greeting was "It's the Doublemint Twins!" (It still is often the greeting of choice, even after all these years.) The two of us would always laugh and pretend it was the first time we were hearing it, even though we have heard it about 17 times a day for most of our lives.

We were each other's peer group. We felt bolstered, reinforced by this generic Xerox, this reflector of all of our complex pleasures and pain. Narcissistic though it was, we felt safe from the evil influences of the outside world, as long as we stuck together. We were sowing the soil for a co-dependency the likes of which sends psychiatrists running to psychiatrists. Our alikeness was a problem that was to grow to gargantuan proportions.

Growing up, we were inseparable, and we shared the same classroom. Today, twins are put in different classrooms, so they can have the experience of developing separate and individual identities, different friends and experiences. We shared the same schoolwork, teachers and friends. Our personalities were so intertwined that we might as well have been joined at the hip. "We're joined at the ego!" we have always joked. This led to a gigantic identity crisis when we were just starting college. Together, we were a force. Divided, we were as helpless as Supergirl in kryptonite pantyhose. A split egg. Half a Rorschach blot. A crippled half-person.

We lived in terror of facing the world alone.

As we grew older, boys came into the picture. And that changed our relationship. Dating caused one or the other of us to feel lonely, and it separated us emotionally. But it was a necessary step in our maturation process.

When we were eleven, Mom and Dad enrolled us in "Cotillion," or ballroom dancing classes. Every Saturday, we looked forward to going as we got to wear pretty dresses, white cotton gloves, nylon stockings with garter belts from Mosteller's and shiny black patent leather flats with clip-on bows. All the little boys had to wear suits and ties, and smelled like their fathers' Old Spice cologne. It was our first scent of the dating life to come.

All the girls sat in a row against one wall, and the boys sat on the opposite wall, shifting uncomfortably in their chairs in the enormous and dark Cotillion room. Our dance instructor Mr. Percy, who wore his hair in a greasy pompadour, called out "Ladies' Choice," all the girls scurried to the boys' side to choose a partner for that dance. Terry would sometimes pick Jimmy Olseski, not because she liked him much, but because he was the only boy that lived near us. She felt safe in the familiarity. But it came with a price. Jimmy munched on potato chips from his coat pocket while they slow-danced. He got Terry's gloves all greasy.

We usually picked the Woolsten twins. They were skinny, pale, dark-haired boys with smiley eyes and they looked exactly alike. Later in high school, they carried Bibles around and quoted passages from the scriptures. They toyed with the idea of starting a cult and asked us to be the art directors for their Utopian Society. (We politely declined, although the idea briefly captured our imagination).

In that dreary lecture hall, we learned the "ancient" dances our parents danced, like the fox trot and cha-cha, as well as the jitterbug. Up, side, together, back. Forward, back, step, step, side, back, step, step. We loved to dance the jitterbug and slow dances to songs like. "Blue Velvet," "Put Your Head on My Shoulder" and "Shangri-la." Mom and Dad loved to dance, too, though they didn't do it often. Whenever they danced they

looked happy, as though they had instantly time-traveled back
to the easier, more carefree days of their youth. We wished they
could always have fun together like that. Marriage didn't seem
like it was too much fun, truth be told. Not like it was on TV,
anyway.

At the end of the class, we were allowed to cut loose with
modern music from The Who or The Doors, The Beatles, and
the Rolling Stones' "Jumpin' Jack Flash." It seemed strange to
be going abruptly from such quaint dance styles to hard-core
rock and roll; it jolted us uncomfortably into the harsh reality of
the present. Once, our science teacher Mr. Prichard surprised us
all and performed with his rock band at Cotillion. Who knew he
was so hip? We weren't ready to grow up; the rock and roll
culture scared us. Our sheltered life did little to prepare us for
the challenges of real life that lay ahead.

Linda Speaks

At sixteen, I dated a tall, blue-eyed boy named Bill. He sang
tenor in the choir; I sang soprano. He was outgoing and fun,
with a ready laugh. During our year and a half relationship, I
discovered he had a sense of humor and intelligence, possessed
a spiritual quality, and had a cynical, mildly rebellious streak
that appealed to me. And to complete the rebel persona, Bill
played rock and roll guitar. He especially liked the Rolling
Stones.

I went to the Senior Prom with Bill. It took me a very long
time to make the gown myself. I loved plaid, and decided I
wouldn't be corny like the other girls with their J.C. Penney
pastels and too many ruffles. My dress would be black and
white PLAID, very haute couture like a Valentino. Back in the
early seventies, nobody wore a plaid evening gown. It was a
very bold move. I looked like a sofa. A skinny sofa. I don't

remember getting a compliment that night, at least not a sincere one. But I felt beautiful, and boy, did I make a statement. Plaid evening dresses did eventually become all the rage… about 25 years later. Even my fashion sense was psychic!

Bill astonished me one day by announcing that he had thrown away his eyeglasses in an impulsive act of faith to recover his eyesight. (Like me, he was nearsighted.) While I admired this bold gesture, I couldn't help but notice he was fumbling around quite a bit, and I wondered just when his little experiment would "take." (Apparently it didn't. He was pictured wearing glasses in our 25th reunion brochure). Bill went to Duke University eventually, and then to Seminary School in New York City. He later became a successful Episcopal priest with a large congregation in Dallas, and we still keep in touch.

Terry Speaks

In high school, our best friend was a wonderful boy named Drew. We met at age fourteen, in English class. We did everything together: singing in chorus, ice-skating on the pond near his home, Christmas caroling, school musicals, bike trips. I went to the Junior prom with Drew, and we had a crush on each other. In college, Drew discovered that he was gay, and even though many of us had suspected this, I cried when he told me. Meanwhile, I had trouble watching Linda drift away, as she began to focus more of her attention on Bill. During summer vacation in Maine, Linda would spend hours writing letters to him, while I retreated into my own reclusive world. That is when my depression really began, an albatross with which I would struggle for decades. Yet while I struggled, there were still some glimpses of the life we would eventually lead as psychics.

We Speak

In seventh grade, Linda scribbled on a little white pad of paper that was beside her bed. For some reason she found herself writing the words "Palingenesis Symposium" and drew a little Angel's face in pre-Raphaelite style next to the words. She had never heard of the word before, and just assumed she had made it up. It was not until thirty years later that she remembered the word "palingenesis" and decided to look it up in the dictionary. To her surprise, it meant "the transmigration of souls" or reincarnation. Perhaps the words and images were prophetic, an omen that we would one day be practicing both Buddhism-- a philosophy that includes reincarnation-- and mediumship. This was her earliest experience of automatic writing.

A few years later, the book The Search for Bridey Murphy, by Morey Bernstein captivated Linda. It was about a woman in the fifties who began to have vivid dreams and memories of a past life in Ireland in the nineteenth century. A compelling true story, it made a strong case for the existence of reincarnation. So intrigued was Linda by this groundbreaking book, she could not put it down. We never did know why our parents had it on their bookshelf, because it wasn't at all the type of book they would read. Although it was quite controversial in its day, Bridey Murphy triggered for both of us a lifelong fascination with the subject of reincarnation. In fact, part of our current work involves channeling specific past lives and their influence on an individual's present life and purpose.

Chapter Five

THE MIRROR HAS TWO FACES

"One does not discover new lands without consenting to lose sight of the shore for a very long time."

- Andre Gide

Terry Speaks

One morning, I woke up in a panic. I thought I was Linda. I felt utterly despairing and hopeless. I was a black hole, a non-person.

My abyss was precipitated by reading The Bell Jar by Sylvia Plath. That is the last book a depressed person should read. Sylvia stuck her head in the oven shortly after writing it. But my depression had started years earlier in high school.

When Linda started dating Bill, I went through what felt like a divorce, trying to establish my own identity, despite my feeling I didn't have one separate from my sister. Shortly after, my headaches started. They were small ones at first, but they came every day. These led quickly to full-blown migraines. By the time I attended art school, the one-two punch of depression and migraines had become my nemesis. Yet I didn't give up on life. It felt like some invisible force wouldn't allow that possibility. I was driven to find a cure or at least some respite from constant pain.

Other art academy students suffered from depression as well. The early seventies was a period of turmoil. We art students especially were feeling a bit lost. In the year and a half we were in Philadelphia, two friends committed suicide.

One of our friends was a very funny yet cynical Jewish girl named Sharon, who had a bushy sandy-colored ponytail, and wore no makeup. We thought she was brilliant. We learned of her suicide through another friend, and it was such a shock, because she had not seemed depressed at all.

Another friend, Bill Stokes, was a tall handsome Texan boy with dark wavy hair that he wore messy and uncombed. He had a kind of X-factor magnetism, and spoke with a slow Texan drawl. He was one of the best painters in the school, and teachers liked him. Yet Bill was humble; he once told Linda that he wished he had her drawing ability. There were rumors of a drinking problem after he killed himself, but no one was sure what happened exactly. After his girlfriend broke up with him one cold winter night, he jumped off the Schuylkill Bridge.

We hadn't had much experience with death, and didn't quite know what to do with the news. He seemed to have such promise, a raw talent that would make a mark in the art world some day. What had gone wrong? That is a question I finally had to ask myself at a low point during this time.

At the time we were seventeen and living at the Roosevelt Hotel in Philadelphia, having recently started our second year at the Pennsylvania Academy of the Fine Arts. Art school was an inevitable choice for both of us; we clearly had watercolor instead of blood running through our veins.

At the Academy, there was intensive training in art history, painting, sculpture, etching, graphics disciplines, and long hours of rendering detailed drawings from life and plaster casts of sculptures. Teachers believed in our talent. We felt at home here.

During my first semester, I had started a friendship with another painter, Mike Cockrill, which soon turned into my first real romance. Mike shared my obsession for painting, and we talked for hours about art: classical art, modern art, minimalist art, conceptual art. We argued about it, gushed over it, analyzed it. Mike was an intense, passionate, and confused young man. During our arguments, he threw chairs across the room. This should be a red flag to anyone who is involved with a violent person: "Beware! Danger ahead!" Beneath his tall, blond, boy-next-door appearance was a very angry, fiercely rebellious spirit.

Yet Mike was also very supportive of my talent in those days. He grasped my potential and encouraged me to become the artist that I am. He was my best friend for many years. I know that Mike was greatly inspired by my work and my lifestyle. For awhile, he adopted a painting style very similar to mine. He idolized my dad's paintings, too. Mike and I were similar in temperament, but I didn't have to work at being rebellious like he did, it was my nature. I felt like Mike had a desperate need to prove that he was a bad boy, like his hero Jackson Pollock, and not "the golf club kid" that people called him in art school. We were a kind of Steiglitz-O'Keefe pairing of the seventies. And yet it worked. That is, it should have worked. But we were too young, and had no communications skills, no real sense of who we were.

I'm not sure exactly what triggered my "breakdown," but something snapped one morning, and I had the first in a series of panic attacks that scared the living Bejesus out of me. I was eighteen, and my anxiety had reached serious proportions. I remember watching "Goodbye, Columbus" on TV and bottoming out. I started crying and I didn't stop for several days.

This is when I woke up the next morning and thought I was Linda. My parents were scared, too. They called our family doctor. "Oh, you're just as bad as my kids," was his insensitive response. He referred me to a psychologist who had no idea what to do with me either. He would talk on and on about himself, not knowing how else to get me to open up. I would stare for hours in a dark room, not moving. I felt utterly paralyzed emotionally. Even Linda couldn't understand what I was going through, and I didn't share much with her at the time.

My psychiatrist suggested it would be best for us to learn to establish individuated identities. "I need to go away to school, and you can't come with me," I told Linda. In the spring, I went away to Penn State at State College, and Linda left for the University of Delaware. It felt as if we were light years apart. We didn't speak for months at a time, both of us trying to gain our footing and begin the long journey toward forging individual selves. Learning to become separately functioning individuals was an absolutely terrifying task, and seemingly impossible.

Linda's roommate in the dorm was, coincidentally, named Terri. This new roommate was bulimic; she binged and purged. She also smoked pot, slept with the TV on all night long, and stole money from Linda's purse. For the sake of sanity, Linda had to move to a private home to rent a room from a family of five called The Andersons. Mrs. Anderson was a neurotic "desperate housewife" in her fifties, with enormous wide-set blue eyes, who would dramatize her marital problems to Linda, and use her as a therapist. Being a compassionate soul, Linda would listen and console her endlessly, reassuring her that life was worth living.

Linda rode her bicycle to campus, even in the rain. One day she didn't see a car parked in front of her path, and she went sprawling over the rear hood of the car, umbrella and school books flying helter-skelter. Adjusting to life without a twin was a real challenge. When we were together, we had always watched out for each other.

Meanwhile, I was on campus at Penn State, calling the suicide hotline. Late at night, I woke up in the cold sweat of sheer panic at the thought of life. Disinterested psychiatrists slid prescriptions for drugs across shiny desks. "Oh, you're just homesick," they told me without looking up from their writing. None of them helped, I just remember feeling numb on antidepressants in philosophy class, unable to make sense of the professors' words. Meanwhile, two of my roommates, both orphans, attempted suicide. It seemed that wherever I went, my karma of being around depression and death followed me.

It wasn't long before I came down with a serious virus that sidelined me for the entire semester. What started as a simple case of mono turned out to also be Epstein-Barr Virus, the precursor to CFS or chronic fatigue syndrome. It is incurable and untreatable, and at the time, doctors did not even know what it was. Later on, while in her thirties, Linda was also diagnosed with Epstein-Barr. I spent six months studying, barely able to make it to classes, and with no social life whatsoever. As miserable as I was, this lifestyle seemed to be the formula for getting straight A's.

But Linda and I were still able to spend the summers together. Somehow, Mike and I had managed to keep our relationship going. In the summer of 1974, we took a job with Mike, doing charcoal portraits on the Wildwood, New Jersey boardwalk. We worked in a place called "Artists' Alley," run by Gary Gibbons. Gary was a jovial bearded man who took half of everything we made. We got to be good at quick portraits and caricatures. Linda excelled at babies' and childrens' portraits, I loved capturing the strong faces of Canadians, their beautiful eyes and sharp cheekbones.

While we were in Wildwood, Linda dated a songwriter named John. He had a couple of hit records in the fifties, Sum-Sum Summertime and The Martian Hop.

Linda really freaked out when one night she caught him sweeping our porch at 3:00 a.m., ranting about being Jesus Christ. That chapter ended abruptly.

On Labor Day, our last day of work for the summer at Artists' Alley, we closed shop and headed back to our car, which we had parked in the lot of a nearby hotel. In the dim twilight, we heard a deep voice cry, "Take one move and we'll blow you away." We turned to see the red glow of two high-powered police rifles pointing at our heads. For a split second, I flashed back to the JFK motorcade scene and imagined my head exploding. Linda gave me a sharp glance. Mike nervously cracked a joke. We were relieved to have put all our cash for the portraits we had done that day in our shoes. It could have looked really bad. We opened our trunk, and there was a wooden box. We all leaned in. The police leaned in. They opened the box. It was full of half-used rainbow-colored Windsor Newton pastels. Turned out someone in the hotel had overdosed and the police thought we were heroine dealers.

A slow crime day in Wildwood, New Jersey.

After a year at Penn State, I transferred to Temple University's Tyler School of Art in Philadelphia. I became even more reclusive and moody, holed up in my room, painting. I was the only student who attended life drawing class. Drawing from the figure had become "passe" by then, and students were more interested in photo-realism, film, or conceptual art. I experimented with many styles of painting, finding that I had an unusually painterly or expressionistic style. I painted self portraits. At least if I killed myself, they'd know what I looked like.

Linda transferred to Tyler, too, and we spent our last semester at Tyler School abroad, in Rome, Italy. I felt as though I had time-traveled to another planet, it was the most beautiful place in the world. We were overwhelmed by the art that we saw in

Italy. We learned to speak Italian and toured the Northern cities, Florence, Venice, Milan. I am sure that experience changed our life. 1976 was a difficult year for us in Rome. We got caught up in a Communist rally, and men with bayonets were stationed outside of our pension. Linda was hospitalized for several days with ptomaine poisoning. The Italian men harassed us, and our health was taking a downward turn.

After my return to the U.S. and my college graduation, I married Mike in a small ceremony in my hometown of West Chester, Pennsylvania. We invited only our immediate families; there were twenty of us in all. Linda and our friend Greg sang "Morning Has Broken" in two-part harmony and I cried as I walked down the aisle. It rained. Mike's mom said later that it was the most beautiful wedding she had ever attended.

After graduating from Temple, Mike and I moved with Linda to crazy New York City. Our life became the bohemian experience that many dream of but could never imagine living. Some of our experiences were like living a dream, but much of it was a desperate nightmare as we fought an invisible war with the darkest forces of our soul. Yet that fight was the single driving force in our spiritual awakening, and ultimately the catapult for our psychic development. On hindsight, I believe it was our mission to survive and show proof of the power of our own spirit and of the universal Source that guides all of us.

Chapter Six

LIVING DOLLS

"I can take reality in small doses, but as a lifestyle I think it's too confining."
— Lily Tomlin as Trudy the bag lady, *The Search for Signs of Intelligent Life in the Universe*

Linda speaks

Art school was a constant frustration for me. While I had a gift for painting and drawing, I didn't appreciate it at the time. My lack of confidence was painfully evident in the many canvases I would paint, wipe out and toss aside. I felt that although I possessed technical proficiency, I had nothing special to say that had not been said already by hundreds of painters who came before me. My family was very wrapped up in painting, but it struck me as an archaic medium. I yearned to do something that had never been done before.

My heart lacked passion for the genre; I was just going through the motions of the classes at school. I felt a bit guilty that I did not really love the act of painting as much as my father and Terry did, and found myself developing an interest in another art form that would become my consuming focus for the next two decades: performing.

In 1978 I was modeling part-time with a small agency, having just graduated from art school. One day I was bored selling a manicure product on the main floor of John Wanamaker in Philadelphia. Because I would stand very still waiting for

46

customers, several people walked by and would stop dead in their tracks.

"Oh, my *God*! I thought that was a mannequin!" they exclaimed. This happened so frequently that I decided if they wanted a mannequin, I would give them one. I froze in place, hands poised, eyes unblinking, glazed. No one paid me any attention, as I was just a mannequin.

Then I moved ever so slightly, a turn of the wrist, a slow pivot of the neck on its axis, then I would freeze again for several minutes. People stopped, mesmerized. "George, did you see that mannequin move?" George would shake his head and make a comment about reducing his wife's medication.

As my amused coworkers looked on, a crowd slowly gathered. My friend, a fellow model, was nearly doubled over in laughter at this point. But I did not move a muscle, perched on my four-inch stiletto heels. Occasionally an unsuspecting shopper would walk by only to become a victim of my ruse and nearly die of cardiac arrest when I batted my eyelashes or turned mechanically on the balls of my feet. I knew I had something here. When I returned home that night, I was very excited in a way that I had never experienced.

The next week, I learned about a contest for all alumni of The Pennsylvania Academy of the Fine Arts, which my sister and I had attended for two years. The contest, sponsored by Lancome Cosmetics, was an invitation to painters and sculptors to submit a piece of art, and the winner's work would be displayed in the window of Bonwit Teller on Chestnut Street in Philadelphia.

I decided to submit myself as a piece of kinetic sculpture.

The day of the submission, I made up my face very extravagantly in avant-garde fashion. I pulled my curly red hair in a severe kind of Parisian punk up-do, wore false eyelashes, geisha-white face powder, magenta lipstick, and an exotic sarong I had designed. Dangling jeweled earrings and a necklace completed the look.

I will never forget the feeling of confidence I had walking through Bonwit's. Only occasionally have I had it since. I knew I would win. I felt excited, powerful, and certain that this was the beginning of something momentous. I entered the office of Carol Firestone, the public relations head, an abrupt businesslike woman who was judging the entries. I saw many works of art scattered around the room: large oil paintings and marble sculptures, a steel mobile hung from the ceiling. There were a couple of plaster casts.

The woman looked up from her disheveled desk, piled high with papers, scheduling books and smaller pieces of art. "Yes?" she asked absent-mindedly, not even hanging up the phone.

"I came to submit my piece of art," I said.

"Where is it?"

"I'm it," I said smiling.

She hung up the phone, and looked at me with considerable interest, as if I were her long lost daughter who had been kidnapped and returned. I knew I had her where I wanted her.

Carefully, deliberately, I took my place in front of her and did my slow-motion transformation from human to mannequin. I proceeded to hold a pose for a minute, then do measured mechanical movements as if motorized. It was an eerie, other-worldly effect with the extreme makeup.

While I moved and blinked in mechanical slow-motion, Ms. Firestone picked up the phone and started dialing madly, inviting each of the heads of Bonwit Teller's various departments to come up to the room. "Call the Channel 4 news, I'm going to have her in the window tomorrow at 10:00 a.m.," Carol announced. "She's unbelievable!"

I was so excited I could hardly believe it. I'd created something entirely new, and launched it commercially. Then I had an idea that would make it even better—my twin sister would be in the window with me.

But Terry was a serious painter and a bit of a recluse by nature. I had never seen her wear makeup or wear a glamorous dress. Her college roommates had called her "The Frump" because she was always in scuffies, a flannel nightie and an old fluffy robe. When I stormed into her Chestnut Street apartment, coincidentally located right beside Bonwit Teller, I was still in costume. Together, we looked like a New Wave version of *The Patty Duke Show.*

I told Terry the news. I think I may have been shouting. Terry was incredulous. She had never considered putting herself on display, had never modeled. She thought I was a bit mentally unbalanced before, but this pretty much confirmed it.

She was scraping at a canvas, but now had turned to face me. I told her that I would teach her the robot mannequin moves, and do her makeup and clothing. It would be fabulous.

Terry looked at me as if I had just told her she was being abducted for alien experimentation. Her protests fell on deaf ears. I knew this experience was going to change the course of both our lives, and set the stage for a career in show business that would span three decades. Within minutes, I had somehow managed to persuade her to do it. I felt like Lucy talking Ethel into a silly scam. I can be very willful when I have an idea.

The next day, my sister and I performed for hundreds of people in Bonwit's window. We were featured in all four Philadelphia newspapers and on three TV news programs. Our lives were altered forever.

Frank Ciosi spotted us doing our mannequin act in Bonwit's. He hired us to work nights at his disco called The Mansion in Wildwood, New Jersey, "down the shore." The Mansion was a tacky club with neon lights, a mirror ball, and packed with Jersey teenagers in too much lycra spandex. He offered us $25 a night. This was more fun than typing insurance forms, so we eagerly agreed. Disco was just starting up, and soon it would be the hottest thing since the jukebox clubs of the fifties. We performed our now-expanded robotic mime and dance act throughout the evening, changing costumes several times a night.

We lived above the disco, and after working we would lie awake while the music pounded until dawn. We shared the tiny room with two go-go dancers. Nikki from Haiti ended up robbing us.

Our boss Frank was a sleazy wheeler-dealer who made a name locally impersonating Rod Stewart, lip-syncing his hits. Every time we saw him he had a different wig on. He propositioned us a few times in the presence of his wife, and was the first of many agents to hint broadly at a "twin" fantasy. He was the second in a long line of Broadway Danny Roses who promised us stardom (Ms. Firestone had been the first). We had grown up in a conservative country town, and we were very naïve, so all of this was sort of a shock. As our popularity grew in Wildwood, Frank added a few performers of questionable talent to create a small "troupe" which he called "Trix."

We landed another gig at Murph and Shirl's "Surf Villa," a small go-go joint near Atlantic City. We were thrilled to be paid to do our robotic mannequin act in between the dancers' sets. We were double-billed with 300-pound "Fat Donna," one of the dancers, whose big (and we mean BIG) finale was stripping to "My Ding-a-Ling." She brought the house down (literally). To our amazement, while we lay on the beach one day, a helicopter flew overhead trailing a banner which read *"300-POUND FAT DONNA AND THE JAMISON TWINS AT SURF VILLA TONIGHT!!"* We laughed till our stomachs hurt.

The highlight of the job was working with Tiny Tim, who starred on the TV series *Laugh-In*, and his wife, Miss Vicky (the two had married on The Tonight Show with Johnny Carson the previous year). Tiny Tim introduced us as "The Lovely Miss Jamison Twins." We couldn't have been more tickled. We got a kick out of the dancers, with their dry "been around" humor. This was the slice-of-life that we loved, the seedy and absurd side of life that most people don't get to experience. It felt very much like vaudeville, or '40s German cabaret, and we were hooked.

A few weeks later we moved to New York City to get a life. Little did we suspect that the great adventures lying ahead for us would rival Harry Potter's.

Chapter Seven

A SERIES OF UNFORTUNATE EVENTS

"Thank you for calling...
If you are obsessive compulsive, press 1 now, as
often as you like.
If you are codependent, please have someone else
press 2 for you now.
If you are schizophrenic, press 3, 4 and 5 now.
If you are delusional, press 6 now, and someone will attempt to
connect you with the mothership.
Or, leave a message at the tone."

- Hugh McKinnon

Terry Speaks

My husband Mike and I started renting a loft in the Chelsea District in Manhattan. Both of us were painting obsessively. There was a serial killer loose known as "The Son of Sam," who was eventually imprisoned for life. Police now have reason to believe he was operating with a Satanic cult. One evening, as we walked from our loft space to Times Square, I began to feel anxious and uneasy. Suddenly, without warning, every single light, sign, and billboard started shutting down as we entered the square. The Winston man stopped smoking. It was the big power blackout of 1977! Pedestrians started directing traffic, looters were smashing windows, chaos reigned. Mike and I ducked into a theater, where Broadway actors stood dazed on the blackened stages; we watched in amazement as theater audiences panicked and bolted for the doors. It was quite a surreal experience to witness. We felt our way home in the black streets, praying that Sam wasn't anywhere around.

New York attracted us for many reasons: it was vibrant, pulsating with creativity, the center of the art world. Were we naive. New York threatened to eat us alive. The late seventies and the eighties were a dangerous time in that city. Violence and robberies were out of control, but all of that changed after we left for California in 1990. On hindsight, I realize we would have been safer in downtown Baghdad. Linda and I were robbed a dozen times in the dozen years were lived there, and we lived in constant fear.

After a year or so, we moved to a huge munitions factory in the Red Hook section of Brooklyn. Mike and I rented a loft in the factory, which became known as the Gowanus Canal Artyard. It was a memorable time of churning creativity. I painted the floor of our loft a bright sky blue enamel. There was a coffee factory next door, and the aroma of slightly burnt coffee always permeated the air. We had no heat in the dead of winter, no kitchen, no solid roof. I washed our dishes in the bathtub. It was as to close to being homeless as it gets. Buckets collected the rainwater, and there were rats in the stairwells. Our art spirit was volcanic. We lived to create, whether it was through painting, performance, collage, costume design, or singing. Noted musician Brian Eno, famous for pioneering the new genre of ambient music, hammered out his music on our bathroom pipes, in the loft space beneath ours. The experimental band Material practiced late into the night.

The day we moved in, our brother Flip helped us move with his pickup truck. Inadvertently, one of us left my cherished photo album out on the landing. After a frantic search, I found all of my photos, including my wedding pictures, ripped twice down the middle, at the bottom of a trash can. The elevator man was psycho, and I guess the happy pictures enraged him. He was fired soon after that, but I didn't take any photographs for many, many years. It did not bode well.

Other artists in the building were Frank Shifreen and Mark Oberg. We collaborated to sponsor "The Gowanus Canal Monumental Show," an exhibition of painting and sculpture featuring New York's emerging talents. I remember hanging a wall of my work next to the work of the famous Keith Haring. People had been comparing our work, but we both agreed that our styles were really quite different. This was the first showing of my paintings, and overall, the show was a great success. Our neighbor Frank had neglected to get permission from our landlord to use the 10,000 square foot space, and he spent the night in jail. We all felt bad about that. But the show received rave reviews which pleased all of us. Linda and I later joined forces with Frank to form our first rock band. We sang Frank's music (Bonkers in Yonkers, Freeze It) and Mike contributed lyrics (Tanks are Expensive, Too Bright for My Eyes). Over the years, Linda and I would sing informally with seven bands. In the mid-eighties we formed the band "Flying Objects" with Jesse Bromberg, and we started writing our own music.

During this time I noticed my intuitive abilities growing along with my artistic ones. I had encouraged Michael Roney to include his eccentric humor in his writing, and he started writing some of his best work. Simultaneously, I had started doing large black and white paintings called The Thorn Woman series. It was my way of channeling my physical pain and depression into whimsical artwork with titles like Buzz Saw Woman and Impalia. Even though I had not yet read Michael's poems, my artwork turned out to be perfect illustrations for Michael's new book, Whistling Jupiter. Again, my psychic gifts were constantly being revealed to me.

But my relationship was deteriorating. Out of the blue one day, Mike admitted to a long-term affair with a designer he had

met. Sadly, we split up, divorcing after nine years together. It
was devastating. It took many years to get over the betrayal. My
closest friend whom I trusted with my life had totally
disregarded my feelings and the vows of our marriage without a
second thought. I packed one suitcase and left, never looking
back. Mike remarried, and still uses that same loft space in Red
Hook as his studio, nearly thirty years later. Despite the initial
shock, I am happier today than I ever was while married to
Mike and have never regretted leaving. But I still appreciate
some of the wonderful times we shared in those early, inspired
years.

My obsession was painting, so when Linda got me into her
"Lucy and Ethel" schemes I resisted at first. But not for long.
Linda was always the more outgoing twin. While I was quite
shy, a part of me yearned for more excitement, and for greater
self-expression. Painting is a very lonely profession. I thrived
on the social interaction that performance afforded me, and I
have always been grateful for Linda's constant inspiration,
encouragement and support. Through the many costumed
personas we created, I discovered myriad aspects of myself that
I never would have dreamed possible.

Linda speaks

When I was twenty, I made a determination to one day "create
a new form of theater" that no one had ever seen before. I did
not have a clue what form this theatrical dream would take, yet I
had a sense it would involve performance art, music and
costume, as these were things that sparked my imagination.

I had lived in Philadelphia for several years as a teenager
while attending art school. I took a modeling course at the John
Robert Powers School, and ended up an instructor there a few
months later. My teacher was a tall, blonde woman of about

forty named Marcy Lacy. She had huge blue eyes like Big Bird, and wore too much makeup. I thought she was great. I loved doing runway work, and teaching young girls how to put on makeup and walk on a runway. My students became my friends. At the end of the course, I designed and made dresses out of yards and yards of pastel cotton gauze for all of the girls, and we had a fashion show for the management and the students' families. It was a total blast. I knew then that my future included design on some level.

For a short time I worked as a retail salesgirl. I later worked in a Mexican fast food joint called Tippy's Tacos. My co-workers were a bunch of pot-smoking hippies, but we had fun.

Moving to New York City seemed a natural thing to do. I loved adventure and fashion and challenges, and being exposed to art and culture on a high level was alluring. Philadelphia seemed too provincial and narrow after a while. Without a dime in my pocket, I packed a few bags and boxes and jumped in the car with Terry and Mike. Flying by the seat of our pants became a way of life for us. In tenth grade English class, I had been voted "Most Likely to Lead a Group of People through the Amazon" because I took risks more than other kids and was a natural leader. It proved to be portentous. New York was like a scary and wonderful jungle to us, and we became addicted to the constant stimulation of art and creativity. Professional dancers in New York City are referred to as "gypsies." As artists, comics, mimes, and singers, we lived like gypsies and were happy with very little in the way of material things. We lived to make art.

I became an adept dumpster diver, collecting found objects and even clothes and hats that I found discarded on the street. I had "an eye", and I was constantly on the hunt for unique and interesting things: curious pieces of furniture, picture frames, mannequins, lamps, appliances, tchotchkes. There was an

absolute need to be hunting all the time. I am still like that.
Every piece of trash had the potential to be part of an art piece
or costume. No matter what town I was in, I would inevitably
find a thrift shop or yard sale with a little treasure meant just for
me to find. Once I even dived head first into a dumpster and
retrieved forty fashion magazines to use the images in my
collages. Terry thought I was a little crazy. She did not share
this obsession. Unlike her, I think of dumpster diving as an
elevated art form.

Terry and I both adored Pop Art. We idolized Andy Warhol,
Roy Lichtenstein, and Robert Raushenberg's huge, splashy,
silk-screened canvases. We even named our performance
company Pop Theatrics. The costumes we made had a bold pop
art feeling, an iconic theme. We considered ourselves to be
playful iconoclasts, poking fun at sacred images and traditions.
We used our art, costuming, poetry, and comedy as a platform
to make wry comments on modern culture.

New York was like a wonderful, wild, scary ride. I took risks
in that city that I would never take now. Terry and I lived in
constant stress; it seemed that we were always struggling to find
work and pay bills. The survival mode took its toll on us and
our already fragile health.

As we mentioned earlier, we had developed co-dependency to
the exponential extreme. Some of our comic characters have
been born from this struggle: Louise, the Two-Headed
Housewife that we portrayed and who was later featured on
Saturday Night Live, is a perfect example of how we used art
and humor to heal the painful identity crisis we were
experiencing. We were surprised to learn in therapy that we had
a classic "symbiosis." This means that our identities were so
entwined that we expected the other twin to behave and think as
we did, as though we were the same person. This is common
with mother-daughter relationships, and in marriages. One of

the things we learned in therapy was to validate and respect each other's feelings and ideas, even if we don't agree. This saved our relationship. Because we have worked so hard on healing our communication, we are now closer than any twins or siblings that we know. It was a very, very hard process, but so worthwhile.

Throughout the fifties and sixties, women were conditioned to search for some means of power, but through finding a husband. Women's lib didn't happen until we were graduating from high school, and girls our age had not been encouraged to have careers. Our parents never spoke to us about marrying or having a career, they assumed we would simply marry at some point, as they had. If women needed to work, they usually opted for either teaching, nursing, or secretarial jobs. Intuitively, Terry and I knew that we wanted to accomplish something meaningful apart from marriage.

We were aware that our mother was totally dependent on our father, and she seemed trapped by the role of housewife. We intuitively sensed her frustration and desire to be more creatively self-fulfilled. Women back in the sixties had few opportunities to explore other options. We both made a decision early on to be self-sufficient, although we had no idea what this might entail. It felt awkward to depend on anyone, either emotionally or financially. I had trouble even letting a man pay for dinner or a movie, because I had difficulty receiving.

Mona Lisa Schultz, in her book *Awakening Intuition*, says that "people tend to be either Velcro or Teflon in temperament, either hanging on for dear life or never bonding to anything." I think, looking back, that I was the Teflon type. I didn't trust men, although I wanted to.

In Italy, at age twenty, I had been date-raped by an Italian man while I was studying in Rome. My roommate at the pensione was dating his best friend at the time, and she introduced me to him. This was such a traumatic experience that I never told anyone about it for seventeen years--not even my sister. It colored my relationships with men for the rest of my life. The deep repression of feelings around the rape undoubtedly contributed to my illness in the years to follow. So out of touch was I with the rage and the shame that I became somewhat driven in my career. I was numb to the pain, completely disconnected from my inner self. Having been raised in an era of pre-psychology, therapy was a relatively new field back then, and very stigmatized. Most people have difficulty sharing their feelings about personal things. The message was always "hang tough" or "keep a stiff upper lip" because in our stoic society, emotions are regarded as a sign of weakness. Sadness and anger are things to be suppressed at all costs. It didn't occur to me that suppressing my emotions might contribute to physical symptoms of disease. Years later, I would learn how to release the pain of the past and create a balanced life. But for years I was locked in a prison of complex emotions and fear, not knowing who to trust, or trusting the wrong people too much.

Chapter Eight

BOOGIE FEVER

*"I can't believe in impossible things!" Alice declared.
"Why not?" said the Queen. "Every day before breakfast I
think of six impossible things. By dinnertime at least half of
them are possible."*

- Lewis Carroll, Alice in Wonderland

We Speak

In the heart of New York's Greenwich Village, we
maneuvered our big thirteen-passenger van through dense
traffic and stopped at the corner of 11th Street and 6th Avenue.
The members of our eccentric and colorful performing troupe
waiting by the curb joked easily with each other, familiar with
this routine, vying for center-stage. Bernard, one of the troupe's
more outlandish performers and our closest friend, was a tall,
athletic and ridiculously funny French Canadian. He swung
down from behind the wheel and swaggered gracefully around
to the back of the van to help load the costumes. We threw the
bulky, lightweight red, yellow and blue bags and boxes into the
back of the van, joking all the while.

This was our entertainment company, Pop Theatrics. We were
an odd mix of New York's finest street performers: mimes,
comics, magicians, fire-eaters, and improvisational comics with
the energy of teenagers, full of pre-show giddiness. Performing
at four parties per weekend, sometimes in three different states,
we were like latter-day vaudevillians in a modern world,
mutants of a sort, trapped in a mystical time machine. We
would descend upon a Bar Mitzvah in the morning, then a

corporate party the same afternoon, beguiling and mesmerizing audiences within a brief four or five hour period, then onto the evening gig at the Plaza, or the Hotel Pierre. It was a difficult life: nomadic, demanding, frenetically energetic and definitely exhausting. But we were the joy-makers, the spinners of fantasy, and we all loved that aspect of the job. One last bag on, and we headed to The Electric Circus, a popular discotheque in midtown Manhattan.

The Electric Circus was already coming to life, pulsing to the steady beat of Sylvester's "Mighty Real." Darkly silhouetted people hung out near the bar, watching the dancing. We made our way to our makeshift dressing room, a tiny upstairs office, with our costumes in tow. Working quickly, we smeared white pancake and eyeliner on our faces and pressed on spidery showgirl eyelashes. Fuchsia glitter was the final touch applied on top of pink lipstick. Costumes of silver satin, lame, sequins and yards of tulle were unzipped from our garment bags and the wrinkles steamed out... they were still damp from the last show.

Annie, or "Lady Bug," was a freckle-faced performance artist and exotic dancer who was also an extraordinary costume designer, specializing in large insect characters. She was squeezing herself into her skin-tight, day-glo green praying mantis costume. Joaquin La Habana, a former dancer with Alvin Ailey, was the prettiest drag queen in the business, in his Carmen Miranda fruit and fishnets, a skirt of bananas flirtatiously circling his impossibly slim hips. Errol Manoff, the famous South African puppeteer on six-foot high stilts, expertly manipulated his marionette puppets from high above the floor. We, the twins, had transformed ourselves into the "Pointed Sisters," gilded android supermodels from another galaxy, mocking haute couture with plenty of attitude. Gleaming gold metallic Mylar cones shot out at angles, cutting into the space around us, from our shoulders and heads and hips. We were the original "Fem-bots," as years later would be portrayed in the Austin Powers movie. Randy and Jimmy, in ape suits and tuxedos, rehearsed their dance act with Danger, a six-foot black glamazon whose body threatened to burst out of her corset boning. Together, we swirled onto the dance floor in a frenzy of neon spandex, Mylar, and marabou, silver capes flying, like a team of extraterrestrial superheroes.

Karen Feinberg defies description. She was Fanny Brice on acid. A brilliantly eccentric comic, Karen was best known for zany characters that she played on stilts, reminiscent of the Queen of Hearts in Alice in Wonderland. As the "Pizza Man," she whirled a huge pepperoni pizza and took orders on a telephone attached to her belt. Karen was our biggest fan. "You're too hot to handle!" she often told us. Together, the three of us sometimes impersonated The Andrew Sisters, singing a medley of '40s songs in three-part harmony.

Our dear friend Bernard Cauchy was a kindred extraterrestrial, a flamboyant carrot-topped performance artist from Quebec. When he auditioned for us, we fell in love with him instantly. Our friendship lasted many years. A bodybuilder at six-foot-four in pumps, his drag nurse character "Miss Selaneous" and his "defective" Russian ballerina, "Ludmilla Sweatalotta," left the guests rolling. He danced for hours with a life-sized doll called "Lulu," designed by Linda and Herbie, which he strapped to his feet. Words can't describe the impact that Bernard and Lulu created, a stunning vision whirling like Fred and Ginger on the dance floor.

We lost Bernard to AIDS some years later, but no one who saw him perform could ever forget him. Shortly before he died, the three of us flew to Honolulu and did volunteer performances for the Honolulu Marathon, the Hilton, and various AIDS benefits. We knew it was his last hurrah, as he had aged very quickly and his symptoms were worsening. We were fortunate to have that time together, and we miss him terribly.

Doug Elkins was our hip-hop boy, nicknamed "White Chocolate" because he was a white guy with the talent of a black street hip-hop dancer. Fluid, almost boneless when he moved. His endless psychedelic stream-of-consciousness patter was always entertaining.

Throughout the night, we cast our spell with great intensity, using mime, precision robotics, improvisational dance and comedy to delight and transform the crowd. The non-stop disco beat of Donna Summers' "Bad Girls" was pounding hard, pulsing through our bodies, the strobes and lasers blinding us. Tony the fire-eater, his black skin gleaming, blew huge fireballs over the heads of the crowd. Throughout the night, we changed full makeup and drag four times, never losing energy.

Then, as suddenly as we appeared, we were gone.

No one has seen anything like this before; they didn't know what to make of this bizarre spectacle. In the era preceding Cirque de Soleil and the Gen X "Club Kids" phenomena, we were the masters of shock value, but we did more than entertain. We were healers all. The objective, if only subliminal, was to elevate the souls of everyone present through theatrical performance and comedy.

For a dozen years, we made our living producing and performing at the biggest special events and parties up and down the east coast. We had created Pop Theatrics after working a year with a company called Le Clique Fantasy Players. We ran Pop for the first year with Ted Shapiro and Linda's boyfriend Herbie Leith. After Linda and Herbie broke up, the two of us single-handedly ran Pop for another decade, producing customized entertainment for corporate and private special events, Fortune 500 companies and all the casinos in Atlantic City. We worked at all the legendary hotels,

restaurants, and casinos, including The Plaza, The Four
Seasons, and The Copacabana in New York and Washington,
D.C., and the Fontainbleau and the Coconut Grove in Miami
Beach. Our company performed at all the hottest clubs in the
scene. In the height of the extravagant eighties, money flowed.
Wealthy clients paid top dollar for our troupe's innovative and
flamboyant "happenings." If a host fancied an Egyptian theme,
we were futuristic Nefartiti's of the Nile. The next night we
would be intergalactic warriors at the Hilton. Most New Year's
Eves would find us entertaining at high-roller parties in the
biggest casinos in Atlantic City: Trump, Bally's, the Golden
Nugget, and The Playboy Club. High rollers are the guys who
win (or lose) at least $100,000 a year, and the casinos throw big
parties to keep them happy. We were brought in as the
improvisational floor show.

We owned, managed, directed, and choreographed the
company without a staff. The four of us learned on our feet
about staging, producing and costuming parties. We were
pioneering an art form that had not yet surfaced in the events
industry, and it was a very exciting time. Most events required
between five and twenty performers. Linda and Herbie would
design and hand-build many of the costumes for Pop, which
were elaborate and larger-than-life, other-worldly. Renaissance
mingling with futuristic. They made huge "Big Heads" (or
character heads) and life-size puppets. Some of the costumes
were over seven feet tall and built from foam rubber covered in
Lycra, held together with hot glue. That hot glue gun went
everywhere with us! God forbid Carmen Miranda would lose
her grapes any given Saturday night! Occasionally, we did lose
our bananas, but that's another story.

We started out doing mostly robotic mime, and gradually
worked up the courage to try out our comedy. Our first comic
characters were a huge hit: Trixie and Dixie Wingding, the

airline stews. We wore baby blue uniforms with matching
pillbox hats perched atop teased platinum-blonde wigs. Barry
Hendrickson, the designer of Cher's wigs, made our wigs. Terry
had inflatable boobs under her dress that she would blow up
with a hose as "a flotation device for the fashion-conscious
flyer." Linda wore a big cast on her arm, due to a "history of
rough landings." We wrote our own material, usually on the
spot, as we danced our way from table to table. At the right
moment, we would launch into our routine. Linda would speak
while Terry pantomimed broadly:

> *"Double over and hug your knees, hold your
> head between your ankles, and remove all heavy
> jewelry and confining clothing. Reach up and
> pull the oxygen mask from the overhead
> compartment, put it against your face and
> breathe deeply, saying ten Hail Mary's and
> remain in a low crouch. In the unlikely event of a
> water landing, your money will be cheerfully
> refunded. Please make sure all children have
> been conveniently stowed in the stow-away bins
> above your seats. And if you need assistance,
> don't bug us—we'll be in the cockpit doing our
> nails!"*

Backstage, we fought about our shoes. It became a running
joke. One of us would invariably forget something crucial to the
costume, and Linda was a consummate perfectionist. Terry used
to swear Linda designed costumes for the Marquis de Sade in a
past life. Once, onstage at the Copacabana, Linda ground her
spike heel into Terry's foot. Terry ripped Linda's wig off. We
were like a couple of feuding drag queens.

We must have done a thousand Bar Mitzvahs (the Jewish celebration of a child turning thirteen) in the '80s. We recall one bar mitzvah that cost $120,000! Jerry Lee Lewis, Count Bassey and His Orchestra and comedian David Brenner were also hired to perform at this opulent affair. Until we hit the scene, a magician pulling a rabbit out of a hat was "de rigueur," and the only kind of party entertainer available. It seems our fantasy circus changed the face of parties in New York City. People yearned for more creative and scintillating events so that their party would be the talk of the town.

Since we began our career impersonating robotized mannequins, we were "voguing" before anyone ever heard of Madonna. We were reed-thin, ghostly white, towering in platform heels, androgynous even in full drag. Because we had cross-dressers in our troupe, audiences took us to be transvestites also. Women peeked down our bustiers to settle a bet. The two of us developed an obsession with illusion. It became our mission to shock, astound, bewitch, baffle, provoke.

From the drag queens, we learned about burlesque comedy, and our humor took on their edge. We shared their irreverent spirit, their love of parody. After a couple of years doing robotic mime and dance, we started to develop speaking walk-around characters such as Louise, the Two-Headed Housewife, who later starred on Saturday Night Live. It wasn't long before we had built a repertoire of twenty original characters. Improvisational comedy became our forte.

We performed for many celebrities including Jackie Onassis, Cher, George Michael, and Donald Trump. President and Mrs. Reagan hired us to produce a show at the White House for 400 diplomats' children. Herbie, Ted and the two of us created a fantasy Christmas event in which we starred. The following year, we were privileged to work alongside some of the old vaudeville greats: Bob Hope, Alan King, Joey Bishop (the only living Rat Packer, at this writing), and Red Skelton. There were times that we shared the stage with Liberace, Pavarotti, and Dionne Warwick. What a great experience, being in such close proximity to these legends. To us, our life was becoming dream-like and surreal.

Through our comic characters, we gave ourselves permission to express feelings of anger, silliness, outrageousness, playfulness, rudeness, sensuality--emotions that our real-life selves censored. It was the only time we truly enjoyed ourselves--when we were taking on another persona, we felt free. We had trouble being happy who we really were without the disguise.

But our performing in an original way was the realization of our dreams. (Remember Linda's vision of creating a new form of theater?) We worked hard to stretch the limits of fantasy and glamour, and the lifestyle was taking its toll on us physically and emotionally. Tragically, many of our performer friends died of AIDS within just a few years. We lost over thirty friends to this dreaded disease, before new medications were created. It was a bit like living through a war. We miss all of them still.

THE BLITZ

One of our most extraordinary opportunities came through a puppeteer friend who introduced us to a producer in London. We wound up as the only female performers in the International Menswear Show in Earl's Court, London! The year was 1980 For two weeks, every single day, we painted our bodies completely from head to toe with silver aluminum body paint, a liquid that was specially designed not to dry. Many people warned us that the woman painted gold in the movie Goldfinger died because her skin couldn't breathe. We did not want this to happen to us.

Linda designed silver lycra swimsuit-style bodysuits and we hired a friend to fabricate plastic belts and collars with chasing L.E.D. lights so that we would look more like robots. We even had antennae that blinked.

Upon our arrival in London, Linda became very ill with an infection, and British Customs officials detained us for hours, grilling us as to why we were in the country. It would be hours before she got to a hospital emergency room. The doctor prescribed medication and the next day she was doing better. We headed to a beauty salon and had our hair cut to 1/2 inch and dyed electric blue. We looked like extraterrestrials, and the silver body paint created the illusion that our bodies were made of molded steel. Over the previous few years, we had perfected our precision robotic movements to such an extent that onlookers actually searched for our motors.

Even in avant-garde London, groups of skinheads taunted us on the street about our blue hair, and shouted insults. Someone actually threw a raw egg at us. But as New Yorkers, we were not strangers to these sorts of reactions to our unusual looks. It rather amused us. This was the "New Romantics Era," and not many had seen a person with blue hair, let alone two alike. We had an androgynous look and played it up by wearing high-tech jumpsuits in shiny plastic, or mens' suits and ties. The following day, we had a futuristic photo session in full body paint with photographer Francis Loney. These photographs, unbenownst to us, would later appear on album covers and magazines worldwide.

The two of us rehearsed long hours with the male models in the show, and it was really thrilliing. We choreographed ourselves in the one-hour spectacle, and it drew hundreds of people from all over the world. People cried out, "Take me to your leader!" and, "Where's your Mothership?"

A charismatic young man with vermillion hair approached us after one of our performances. He introduced us to his five band-members, all part of a performance troupe called "Shock." What was amazing was that two of the group performed in a very similar robotic style to our own. We felt we had connected with kindred souls.

Shock invited us to join them to tour southern England with a Scottish rock band called "Breaker." We quickly became the new darlings of the British underground, being invited to make an unprecedented appearance at the famous Blitz nightclub, supposedly owned by David Bowie, where no Americans had ever performed before. Years later, people would tell us "You two are a legend in London." It delights us that we now have a growing reputation in England as psychics and have been featured regularly on TV, in film documentaries and magazines all over the United Kingdom.

*

Chapter Nine

WILD LOUISE

"Two heads are better than one."

- Louise

We had been improvisational comics for about ten years when film director Maxi Cohen discovered us. Our video artist friends Ellen and Linda Kahn (known as "TwinArt") introduced us. Maxi included us in her documentary "Twin Night," which was filmed at an event for sixty sets of twins at the New York restaurant El Internacionale. We were among several sets of twin entertainers for the party. As a result of that film, which won some national awards, Maxi was hired to make a short film for *Saturday Night Live.*

Most people know that *Saturday Night Live (SNL)* is the longest running comedy show in history. The early years are legendary for having launched the careers of many famous talents, including Bill Murray, Dan Akroyd, Jon Belushi, Gilda Radner, Jane Curtin, Martin Short and Billy Crystal. When Maxi pitched us as the stars of a short film for *SNL*, we were ecstatic. None of the comics in town could get a gig like this. We spent several months rehearsing and preparing for "Louise's Tidy Tips," a three-minute film that aired on *SNL* in 1986, with Sigourney Weaver hosting the show.

We starred as "Louise," the two-headed housewife. Jan Oxenberg wrote the script, and adapted the character from the two-headed lady persona that we had created some eight years earlier for party work. We had called our original character "Phyllis and Harriet." She was big, bold, bawdy, and would say and do anything she liked. An army of stylists and costumers recreated our costume, transforming us from the two-headed Phyllis and Harriet with purple hair into a stylish modern day housewife with, well, two heads. We wore a pink sweater, a spray of butterfly broaches, and blonde Marilyn Monroe style wigs, that flipped up on opposite sides.

Louise had her own TV family: a husband, a small son and a surly punk-rocker daughter with spiked hair. She filed everything in the house by alphabet, while dispensing household tips, dancing to lively salsa music, and keeping up with the children.

The film was shot in one day, in a rented suburban home in New Jersey. We had to wear that damn foam-rubber costume for twenty-four hours straight. The bathroom breaks were a nightmare; we could not get out of the costume so we had to be very inventive. It was like wearing a couch. The producer marveled at our energy level, because some scenes required as many as thirty takes. We filmed into the wee hours of the morning.

It was worth it. "Louise" was a hit.

Five years later the HA! Channel hired us to make a spin-off mini-series of Louise, and flew us from Los Angeles to New York to tape the segments. The miniseries aired in rotation for over a year. Louise can still be seen on the Comedy Channel re-runs of *SNL*. Even today many people we meet remember the two-headed housewife. We were to make history as the only twins to appear on *Saturday Night Live* in three decades.

Chapter Ten

HELLO FROM HELL

"You've got to jump off cliffs all the time and build your wings on the way down."

- Ray Bradbury

We Speak

In the late eighties, we lived apart because we felt the need to develop more independence. At the time, we had not mastered communication with each other, and the stress of working together was causing us to bicker. Terry lived alone in Harlem; Linda was in various digs from Hoboken, New Jersey to West 55th Street in Manhattan. As artists, we were always struggling financially, and to make matters worse, our health was a constant concern.

Since our high school years, we had endured unspeakable pain: migraines that nearly killed us, arthritic back, neck and joint pain, crippling depression, constant infections, and chronic fatigue. An army of doctors gave up on us, but not before misdiagnosing us with a slew of illnesses including mercury poisoning, Marfans Syndrome (a connective tissue disorder), Lupus and rheumatoid arthritis. One NYU pain specialist told us we would go blind and be dead by age thirty of heart failure. Another doctor told us that every organ in our bodies was operating on the level of cancer. A respected herbalist said that Terry was one of the four worst cases that he had seen in all his years of practice.

Over the course of several decades, we were correctly diagnosed with migraine headaches, fibromyalgia (a form of arthritis), IBS, Epstein-Barr Virus or CFS (Chronic Fatigue Syndrome), TMJ syndrome, Interstitial Cystitis, mercury poisoning, and neutropenia, a very rare blood disease which causes a severe deficiency of white blood cells. Later, we were diagnosed with skin cancer and Linda with cervical cancer. Most of these diseases are incurable, some congenital, and we had them all at once. Years passed before we could find any relief from the myriad symptoms. It is truly amazing that we are still walking around in one piece…or, rather, two pieces. One doctor called us "walking miracles."

Finding any treatments for our mysterious pain was a huge challenge, as few existed then, and are still today only in developmental stages. It was pure hell. We wanted to give up living for a long time, although we rarely spoke of it. We both knew that we could and would not abandon the other. We felt, as anyone would, that a life with this many impossible difficulties was not worth living. But our unflagging faith kept us going against all odds. The motto "Never give up-- no matter what!" has been the running theme of our lives.

"You'll be tested severely before you're done… This is your training. Pain can purify the mind and body..." goes a quote from The Way of the Peaceful Warrior by Dan Millman. "A warrior doesn't seek pain, but if pain comes, he uses it."

We tried every form of medical treatment, but none of them worked. Drugs made us worse, and had too many side effects. Alternative treatments offered little more than temporary relief. We experimented with Chinese medicine, classical homeopathy, chiropractic, and countless special diets. We pursued the psychosomatic aspect of our conditions. We tried traditional therapy, Gestalt therapy, rage therapy, hypnosis. Then we delved into the human potential movement: EST, The Forum, Lifespring, and Neuro-Linguistic Programming (NLP). All these modalities contributed something to our self-awareness and many have valuable benefits. We worked with fifteen different shamanic healers, some of them famous. (We will later tell you the story about one of them in the chapter Jacob's Ladder).

One of the most severe ailments we shared was TMJ syndrome (Temporomandibular Joint Syndrome). When we were in our twenties, a dentist in Brooklyn who specialized in TMJ felt that our headaches were due our teeth not growing in fully, which put great stress on the nerves and muscles around the jaw. He advised us to have all of our lower teeth crowned so that they were twice their original height. The goal was a normal "bite." We underwent extreme dental processes that proved to be more pain producing than relieving for us. The original work was done wrong, resulting in extensive problems.

Specialists at UCLA had to redo what the original dentist had done wrong. Linda had to have full lower mouth reconstruction twice over the following eighteen years, which led to multiple abscesses, many teeth breaking off, and constant emergency visits to dentists. Linda spent twelve hours in a dental chair in one day having all her lower teeth restored at once. It was an agonizing process. She subsequently needed two more complicated surgeries to repair the surrounding bone, during which she had to stay totally awake.

Despite not finding answers to our chronic conditions, we never gave up. We felt our practice of Buddhism during this time enabled us to persevere through these severe challenges. Twenty years ago we began practicing Nichiren Daishonin's Buddhism, which consists of the daily chanting of "Nam-Myoho-Renge-Kyo," study of the philosophy and helping others in their practice. We attended our first meeting in New York City, and quickly became quite active in the organization, which is called SGI-USA. This group is considered one of the world's largest world peace movements, with over 12 million members worldwide. Despite our personal struggles and, perhaps because of them, we became volunteer leaders, devoting our time to learning and sharing this wonderful philosophy with others. While this is an extremely difficult practice to maintain, we feel that it ultimately protected us from harm and helped to steer our course in the direction of our highest happiness.

Yet these positive changes came very gradually. We still had to deal with everyday earthly problems, especially living in New York. Although we were determined to stay true to our paths as artists, we found paying the sky-high rent in the eighties very challenging. We moved more times than a nomadic tribe, usually ending up in factory loft spaces (not exactly the trendy remodeled versions). We lived in Brooklyn Heights, Brooklyn depths, Red Hook, Soho, the West Village, the East Village, Tribeca, Jersey City and Hoboken, New Jersey. It was a dangerous time in New York, muggings were commonplace, and we never felt safe for a minute.

Terry's apartment in Harlem was on a very bad corner, busy with drug dealers at all times of the day and night. She used to step over two or three junkies in the foyer just to get in or out of the building. Thieves broke into her apartment twice. On one such occasion, three men broke through her kitchen window and confronted her in broad daylight. They took everything that wasn't nailed down, but luckily did not harm Terry.

Some nights she couldn't go home at all because the gangsters blocked her door, marking their "turf." One night there was a machine gun fight outside of Terry's building. On the subways, we witnessed more gunfights, police chases and muggings. During our years in New York, we were robbed at least ten times. We feel that our strong faith protected us during these horrifying incidents.

Looking back, it's a miracle that either of us survived such a chaotic life. Fortunately, we always had each other and the support of our fellow members. But this kind of adversity makes you very strong. There is a Buddhist symbol of a lotus flower blooming in the muddy swamp. Despite the sludge of our enormous obstacles, we eventually moved to better environments and were able to blossom into the women we are today. We feel we are alive and thriving today because of it.

A Buddhist leader told Linda during the most severe trials with her many surgeries that all fear is ultimately a fear of death. She was able to persevere with more courage by embracing the fear of pain and appreciating the process, however arduous. When you are ill, you are forced to expand what you thought you were capable of being. We both realized that through acceptance, we could find a sense of joy and purpose in our lives in spite of living with chronic pain. Anyone who suffers chronic illness or pain must at some point come to terms with the illness itself and make a peace with it. We refused to let the pain win, fighting to overcome our negativity on a daily basis.

Laura Hillenbrand wrote the novel Seabiscuit while housebound with debilitating CFS, chronic fatigue syndrome. She has suffered with the illness for 17 years. Hillenbrand said that telling the triumphant story of the broken racehorse who becomes a champion was "wonderfully therapeutic." Writing the book became her lifeline. "It was so freeing to step out of my body and attach myself to a powerful creature," says Hillenbrand. She also identified with Red Pollard, a failing jockey who, despite partial blindness and broken bones, rode the horse to victory. "Red and I have something in common—the frailty of our bodies, she says. "I understood his frustration and pain and his willlingness to sacrifice his well-being to achieve something."

As Buddhist leaders, we discovered a new sense of purpose
that we were meant to teach, inspire, and motivate others. Over
the last twenty years, we have been able to parlay this into a
thriving career, counseling people all around the world.

New Age Rage

Radionics
High colonics
Psychic healings
My head's reeling

Buddhist moanings
and ear conings
Algae fasting
Facial blasting

E.T. abduction
Liposuction
Toxic shame
Who's to blame?

Cranio-sacral
Where's the Nyquil?
My inner child's
Gone plum wild

Pleiades and
Pass the peas
Tai chi, yoga
Where's my toga?

Ayurvedics
Oy, my headaches
Deepak Chopra
Next on Oprah

Chinese herbs
I'm so perturbed
Seaweed, kelp--
Somebody, help!

Rice basmati
Leave your body
Pranayama
So's your mama

Toxic metals
Soup with lentils
Free your spirit
But don't get near it

Low-carb diets
Causing riots
Astral traveling
I'm unraveling

I'll be enlightened
When I'm through--
What's a New Age girl to do?

- Linda Jamison

Chapter Eleven

UNDERTOW

"Where there is no hope, one must invent hope."
- Albert Camus

We Speak

By 1990, after more than a dozen years in New York, we were tired of starring in this one-act drama. Without being quite sure why, we felt an irresistible pull to move across the country to Los Angeles. Little did we know that the play had a second act.

The week we were to fly to Los Angeles, Terry's boyfriend Edwin informed us that Federated Department Stores, who owned Bloomingdale's, had filed Chapter 11--bankruptcy. Our hearts sank. We had provided two weeks of Christmas shows with twenty entertainers for them, and they hadn't paid us. We lost all the money we had earned: $16,000. Operating on pure instinct, we flew to California with a couple of suitcases and less than two hundred dollars in our pockets.

Starting out in "The City of Angels" was extremely difficult for us. No money, no jobs, no car, no contacts. We didn't even own a television! We started doing our psychic readings, but didn't charge for them yet. Terry took an endless procession of odd jobs, working for doctors as a temporary assistant, and eventually running an acupuncture clinic and a private elementary school. In fact, she provided secretarial work for most of the surgeons now starring on "Extreme Makeover." Linda's first job was hand-beading and decorating bridal gowns. She also did secretarial and reception work. Her forté was retail clothing sales; she became a top salesperson for Guess, Armani, and Tommy Hilfiger. It was the only time in our lives that our career paths diverged.

We both felt imprisoned in the claustrophobic office jobs, and we held onto our dream of performing comedy work. Ultimately, we wanted to have our own TV show. We were prepared to "wing it" just as we had always done. We eventually bought an old beat-up car for $500, drove without car insurance, and did trades for luxuries like massages and haircuts. Yes, a haircut was a luxury item. To make ends meet, we shared small one-bedroom apartments for years, continued to do all of own secretarial work, booking, and public relations, which saved us thousands of dollars. We got free advertising through TV coverage or magazine articles. We made our own clothes and costumes for a fraction of the retail value. For shows and special events, even for TV or film appearances, we did our own makeup. We cooked most of our meals at home, rarely eating out.

To this day we still do most of these things. It has paid off. We have never been in debt, while many of our friends who had sizable incomes have gone through bankruptcy.

Pain was still a constant in our lives and so most of our earnings still went to doctors and dentists, specialists or healers. We had no health insurance for many years; insurance companies would reject us on the basis of "pre-existing conditions."

This was frustrating because we wanted so much to be a powerful example of faith to people we knew, yet it took many years of prayer to show results in our health. At times, we did not think we could go on fighting. It felt as though we were wading through mud. We learned to embrace our obstacles, appreciating them as an opportunity to grow. "Winter always turns to spring," the Buddha Nichiren Daishonin wrote. Our faith encouraged us to change the poison into medicine and transmute the pain.

Los Angeles had its own disasters. In our first three years there, we experienced the Malibu fires, which engulfed the city with billowing black smoke, the South Central riots, and El Nino flooding. One cold January morning in 1993, we were jolted awake by one of the largest earthquakes in U.S. history— the Northridge Quake. We literally thought we were going to die. It felt as if a giant had grabbed our house with gargantuan hands and started shaking it. Yet compared to living for twelve years in the ghettos of New York, these challenges seemed like minor problems for us. Frankly, we half expected swarming locusts to descend upon us. That didn't happen. But it would have been easier than what we were about to endure.

Linda speaks

Late in the year 2000 we were diagnosed with cancer on the same day, by two different doctors. I was diagnosed with cervical cancer. On the same day, another doctor discovered that Terry had skin cancer. Fortunately we both went through successful surgeries. But it was a wake-up call for us. Our dear friend Conner had just committed suicide, so we were in a somewhat fragile state emotionally. My gynecologist called to say she had found extremely abnormal cells (dysplasia) in my most recent Pap smear. A second doctor's opinion revealed that it was Stage 4 cancerous cells, and I was told that I must have surgery immediately to prevent it from going into the uterus. My homeopathic physician tried to convince me to hold off on the surgery, and to try to work with homeopathic remedies. But it seemed too urgent to try to treat with alternative therapies. I knew that millions of women die from cervical cancer every year, and I did not want to be a statistic. After much chanting and deliberating, I decided to undergo a LEEP procedure the following week. It was a difficult recovery, but the surgery was successful. Since then, abnormal cells have continued to recur, which has required yearly biopsies. But I am very confident that with faith we can both overcome the tendency to develop cancer.

People often ask us if we are psychic all the time, or if we can "turn it off" at will. I had a funny experience at the gynecologist's office during my second-opinion visit for cancer. It proves that we are psychic pretty much all the time. I had been referred to a father-son OB-GYN team in Westlake Village, the doctors Carlson. The younger Dr. Carlson was affable and talkative, and he was the one to do my exam. When I was lying on my back with legs in stirrups, he started to ask me about what I do for a living. I replied that I was a psychic. This fascinated him, but admitted he was skeptical. "Sooooo... let's see," he said, probing with his speculum. "If you are psychic, maybe you can name the only mammal besides a human that can be cultured for the leprosy virus." I stared up at the ceiling in my paper gown and tried not to think about the exam. Immediately I envisioned a very clear picture of an armadillo.

"An armadillo?" I said, certain that I must be wrong. It seemed improbable.

"Oh, my God, you really *are* psychic!" He exclaimed loudly enough for a nurse to hear and open the door. "Helen, go get my father. She just said armadillo! He won't believe this! I'm impressed!"

"I told you I was psychic," I said, laughing on the cold table. "I do some of my best psychic work on my back, during gynecological exams."

"I'm going to get you clients!" he said. Another skeptic converted.

Meanwhile, we both were struggling with migraines, and they were getting worse. Terry's headaches would last up to three months at a time, and she ended up in the hospital. Doctors said she nearly had a stroke. Medications failed to bring us any relief from the pain and fatigue. Terry would tell me how she would emerge from a migraine episode feeling an extraordinary sense of clarity. She would be able to continue with her psychic work, even demonstrating her psychic abilities on national television, in spite of having the most incredible migraine headaches.

To compound this complex situation, we were both involved in two major car accidents. In both cases, we were hit from behind by large trucks, causing whiplash. The doctors and nurses called us "The Traction Twins" in the hospital, both of us side by side with our heads in traction devices! In the late'90s I developed chronic mysterious fevers and symptoms that my doctor said exactly mimicked malaria. Yet testing showed it was not malaria. The constant achiness in my muscles and joints, combined with extreme fatigue and swollen glands was almost unbearable, and lasted for many years. But I absolutely refused to give up.

We speak

Since it took us decades of work to break through in our career, clients respected us for that. They often called us for advice about their startup business or invention. We told them there are five basic elements that you need to succeed: money, time, patience, support, and commitment.
We ourselves were seriously lacking in some of these areas, as most people are, but we learned to strengthen our weaknesses as we went along.

We invested in ourselves and each other, and it paid off. We started our first business in our early twenties with no seed money at all. While none of our businesses failed, we initially didn't make much money doing what we loved. Today we are still self-employed and thriving. But the freedom to work as artists came at an enormous sacrifice of being financially insecure and living frugally for years.

People thought we had money. But due to our constant illness, which affected our ability to work for months at a time, our income was up and down. Whatever money we did have went to paying medical bills. We were so poor for so long, we used to shop at the 99 cent Store, outlet stores and Goodwill. When we first appeared on television, we had to borrow the outfits we wore from a friend. We got in the habit of sharing every single thing we bought, sharing one car, and the same apartment; we even shared our dinners when we ate out at restaurants. This amuses our friends to no end, because we still do this today. That is why we are so skinny. Naturally thin? Hell, no! For years we couldn't afford to eat!

What we lacked in money, we made up for in faith. We had not been raised with the belief that we were free and powerful enough to create our own reality; we began reading New Age books and became fascinated with the idea that we humans have boundless potential to create the lives we want. It is a difficult concept for many people to grasp, partly because many of us feel guilty or unworthy of such a life. Most of us don't realize that we have these options.

We have found that many who seek readings from us have a dream of fame and fortune, but they are not willing to do the work or make the necessary sacrifices to get there. This is where the old adage "You can't get something for nothing" applies. We get a lot of calls from people all over the country who want magical solutions to big problems. They refuse to get jobs if it isn't their "dream job," and they don't want to take reasonable action to attain their goals. We try to encourage them through our tenacious example.

Our spiritual practices taught us to dream big. But you need to make the dream into a goal, take action on it, and never give up until you win. Some of the airy-fairy metaphysical books on the market talk about how if you pray, you can get anything you want. This is simply not true. While we believe in prayer, it is the right action coupled with prayer that brings results. We have found that the Universe always answers our prayers, and sometimes the answer is "no." It is for a good reason, a reason that may not at first be apparent to you. Our practice helped us to strengthen our faith and determination, despite not seeing visible results right away. If we had let life's circumstances bombard us, we might have felt like victims, powerless to change our fate. Fortunately, we developed trust in our intuition. We could see which opportunities were worth taking. We were creative enough to be flexible. We changed our goal, if necessary. We rewrote our life script. If there was "no cheese down one hole," we tried another hole.

Many people either give up or keep going down the hole with no cheese. We help our clients see their own potential and different options available that they cannot see. We then offer empowering tools for growth and change to get them to the next step. If they use these tools, they ultimately realize their dreams. A wise man once said that if opportunity doesn't knock, build a door. We built many doors along the way to realizing our dreams, and we have dedicated our lives to helping others open their own doors of possibility. In the last chapter of this book, we will talk more about how you can develop your psychic gifts, and open the doors to your future.

Chapter Twelve

ALMOST PERFECT

"This life has been a test. If it had been an actual life, you would have received actual instructions on where to go and what to do."

- My So-Called Life

Linda speaks

Since my childhood, I suffered from chronic, acute, bizarre infections that doctors had never seen before. I became more and more convinced that I would never be able to do what normal people do-- engage in sports, hold a steady job, get married, have children.

On a deep level, I felt inadequate. I was Type A to the tenth power. This led to a compensating obsession with being the best in everything. Perfectionism is a suffering beyond striving for excellence. It is a need to be perfect, or else not engage at all. The idea of a balanced life never occurred to me. I was hugely ambitious and possessed a fiercely adventuresome spirit. But I was constantly driven to attain an impossible ideal.

For example, after my performances, I would often focus on the one thing that was not perfect, rather than celebrating the fact that I had created a wonderful fantasy for people. This caused me a lot of anguish which then resulted in more physical pain. Pain controlled my life. It was so powerful and the fear so overwhelming that a part of me just went numb. I found that resisting the pain was no help. Dr. C. Diane Early writes in *The Woman's Book of Creativity*: "The first step in recovery comes when the perfectionist recognizes the damage she is inflicting upon herself and decides the price is too high."

Dr. Christiane Northrup describes perfectionism as "having an extreme need for external order to cover internal chaos." A perfectionist's greatest fear is being flawed, making a mistake, or losing control and therefore being unacceptable or somehow unworthy of taking up space in the room. It's a bit like finding yourself on the spin cycle at the Laundromat, spinning eternally, and never getting to final rinse.

Over the years, I learned to forgive myself for any perceived weaknesses or failings, and accept myself as I was. I decided to honor the karmic laws that made such a difficult experience necessary. I learned that in loving the process, we expand on an energetic level. We allow for an unconscious shift and a healing to take place that may have been impossible in a contracted state. In my case, my contraction was resenting my physical pain. I was learning compassion for myself.

My perfectionism had damaged my relationship with Terry. I pushed her away by criticizing her. Her flaws became a mirror for mine. If everyone is our mirror, how much more so for identical twins! Luckily for her, Terry is not as much of a perfectionist as I am, and has always been more accepting of her humanness. Terry and I would get into power struggles over the slightest things. Therapists helped us sort it out, and we encourage twins and siblings to learn empowering communication tools.

I think that I had created illness as part of my "sacred contract." A sacred contract is one that is made prior to birth to experience certain lessons here on earth and heal from them. In accepting the higher purpose of my pain, I became free. I decided to love my imperfection and accept my process, even though it was difficult, uncomfortable and even agonizing at times.

I realized I had to let go of attachment to the outcome of my actions. Many of us have a lot invested in being perfect, healthy, and strong. But how are we feeling while we are striving for the perfect result? Are we enjoying the moments that lead up to a desired end? Christopher Reeve and Michael J. Fox had to learn this lesson in their struggle with chronic illness. Both men became extraordinary leaders in pioneering cures. Christopher died a hero. Michael still continues to fight his battle with Parkinson's Disease, saying, "It sucks... I'll give the disease as much attention as it needs, but I won't give it as much attention as it asks for."

We have to love ourselves as much as we can, wherever we find ourselves. That can be really hard! Yet deep inside of us we can access a knowing that it will all work out. I return again to that Buddhist metaphor about the lotus flower blooming in a muddy pond. We focus so much on the muddy pond, we can't see the Lotus flower blooming. We can't see our innate Buddhahood blossoming. I have learned to embrace the negative points of my life, appreciating the many gifts that I do have.

One very wise friend of ours once said, "There is something wonderful and powerful about your life. When you really feel this, something changes. Then healing becomes possible."

Chapter Thirteen

KIDS, DON'T TRY THIS AT HOME

"The number one rule is, there are no rules."
- Ed Rusha, painter

A normal day is simply not normal for us. Being The Psychic Twins is like living in a constant Reality TV show. Every interaction has the potential to become performance art. One day a woman and her husband approached us in Ikea in Burbank, while we were shopping for kitchen items.

"I have an identical twin too! She lives in Phoenix," said the woman, who was in her early fifties.

"How wonderful!" Linda replied. "But your hairstyles are completely different."

"How did you know?" The woman asked, looking surprised.

"We're psychic. We're known as The Psychic Twins."

"If you're psychic... do I have any children?" the woman asked. Linda was being tested.

"You do." Linda said.

Clearly astonished, the woman pressed for more. "How many?" She challenged.

"You have five. Your twin sister has four," Linda replied as she inspected a ceramic vase.

"Oh, my goodness!" The poor lady turned white as a ghost, and her husband started laughing, enjoying the whole thing enormously.

Terry chimed in, "And you have two grand-children, a girl and a boy. Your daughter is pregnant with a third child." At this point, the startled woman began to back away.

With a twinkle in her eye, Linda said, "Oh, by the way, did you find the bistro set you were looking for?"

This was simply too much information. The couple stammered a goodbye and left quickly. Just a normal day at the mall!

Once we were on a plane flight from LA to New York to star in a British documentary called "Extreme Twins." A pretty, young Asian girl was seated next to Terry, and they struck up a conversation. Terry told her that we were psychics on our way to film a documentary. Linda excused herself to go to the restroom, and the girl pumped Terry for psychic information about her relationship. Terry was a bit hesitant, as she really wanted to relax, but found herself giving the girl elaborate advice about her boyfriend. "You think he's the one, but he isn't. He's too scared of commitment. You'll date about six more months and then break it off." The girl looked startled, disbelieving. "Go ahead," Terry said. "Ask my sister when she comes back from the restroom. She'll say the exact same thing."

Linda came back and sat down. Sure enough, the young lady wanted a second opinion.

"Your sister just gave me a reading about a relationship. I want to know what you think."

As though taking the baton from Terry, Linda immediately started speaking. " I see you in a relationship now, but he isn't the one, though you think he is. You are engaged, aren't you?" The girl nodded. "Unfortunately," Linda continued, "you will separate in about six months." Needless to say, the girl was speechless! She reluctantly admitted that everything we had said was in fact true, and she had been considering breaking up with him if he didn't shape up!

Shortly after our move to L.A., we were sitting in a charming little restaurant called The Rose Café in Venice Beach, when Linda began to write some messages on a paper napkin. The words and phrases flowed, and before long she was writing more and more detailed information in what we later learned was a "conscious trance." The language seemed almost archaic in character, as if it were coming from a being who lived many centuries ago. When we got home, we both decided to experiment more with this "channeled writing," or "automatic writing" which we had never heard about before. In the days and months that followed, the two of us became almost obsessive about writing.

We practiced predicting for friends on many topics: moving, the purchase of a home, boyfriends coming in or going away, jobs. At first, we received information about simple things, mostly, along with spiritual guidance. Soon, people were calling from all over the country for our predictions, which more often than not came to pass. This surprised us as much as it did them, but eventually we came to trust our abilities more and more. As we practiced, we became better at discerning whether the information was coming from a place, or a spirit being (non-physical energy), or from our unconscious or subconscious minds. Terry remembers one young woman who phoned her from Las Vegas. She had lost her wallet in the casino. Terry told her to relax, she had misplaced her wallet in her hotel room. The girl returned to her hotel room and there was the wallet!

The Rose Café was the birthplace of our journey with automatic writing, the technique that we still employ as our main tool for doing psychic predictions, nearly twenty years later. We often give workshops instructing people in the technique of automatic writing.

Chapter Fourteen

ELIMIDATE

Some enchanted evening, you will see a stranger
You will see a stranger, across a crowded room.
And somehow you know
You know even then.
That somewhere you'll see him
again and again.

- Oscar Hammerstein II

We Speak

People often ask us, "Why are you two still single? You're so attractive!"

As you might expect, our dating life has been as bizarre as our career life. We have kept mascara longer than we kept boyfriends. Linda, who was an Avon lady as her first job during high school, used to say that dating men was a lot like selling Avon. A ding-dong here, a ding-dong there, and a lot of wasted samples. In the years after her marriage, Terry dated a British rock drummer, a Jamaican rapper, a Mormon chiropractor, a Navy Seal, a Hawaiian graphics designer, an Italian photographer and a Persian engineer. Linda, not to be outdone, has had three broken engagements and her boyfriends have included a mime and juggler, a classical guitarist, a Jack Nicholson impersonator, a French muralist, a TV set designer, a computer animator, a TV producer, an acupuncturist, and a channeler of the Pleiadians. Together we've dated a set of identical twin magicians (they did a disappearing act) and twin bodybuilders who looked like two Arnold Schwarzeneggers.

What can we say? We like variety.

People often ask us if we played tricks on our boyfriends. In fact, we did once play a joke on someone Linda dated in college. While at Penn State, a friend of Terry's asked Linda out on a date. When Walt showed up at the dorm, Terry pretended to be Linda and Walt fell for it. When he learned the truth, he was terribly embarrassed and we felt so bad about it that we never played another joke! Walt never called again.

Out of that experience we thought of a great idea for a reality show: similar to the series The Bachelor, where all the women are identical twins but the guy has no idea that they are all switching on him. Instead of twenty women, he's dating forty!

Together, we are definitely seen as a force to contend with. Many men have been threatened by the fact that we had the talent and courage to start and manage our own businesses. It seemed that the more successful and better known we became, the harder it was to get a date. And our psychic abilities only added to the problem. Men don't like dating a woman who can read their minds. Can you imagine how scary dating psychic twins would be? A man couldn't lie about anything. We always know when someone is lying to us.

Our dates have fallen into three categories, the "Runners," the "Glommers," and "the Glom-and-Run" types. The runners dash out of sight because they are terrified of intimacy or of women in general. The Glommers are also afraid; they glom onto us like we're their long lost mommies, making dramatic proclamations of love and devotion. Then the Glom-and-Runs do both: they get attached to us, then abruptly disappear. There is a popular dating book called He's Not That Into You, by

Greg Behrendt and Liz Tuccillo. Based on our experience, we're glad some guys aren't that into us.

A funny thing happened to Linda when we first arrived in Los Angeles and she was working in a posh Rodeo Drive clothing store. One of the male shoppers overheard someone say that she was a psychic. Immediately defensive, he challenged her in front of her coworkers to a test: if she could guess the exact color and brand of his underwear, he would take her out to dinner. Always up for a challenge, Linda confidently remarked that he was wearing black Calvin Klein bikini briefs. The man turned five shades of red, stammered something and knocked over a display as he hastily beat a path out of the store. Evidently, he was too shocked to make good on his promise of dinner.

To give another example of the trials of being a psychic in the dating scene, the following story is again absolutely true. Linda had had enough of men fearing her psychic abilities and then leaving skid marks. What is it about the word "psychic" anyway? She wondered. Does it conjure up images of hexes and spells? Potions and animal sacrifice? Did men imagine that we could X-ray their jockey shorts? Or telepathically audit their IRS records? (Well, okay, we can.)

Notwithstanding, she decided to meet people through the Internet personals and not mention that she had psychic ability until they had gotten to know each other rather well. That way, it might not come as such a shock or threat. A good friend found the personal ad of a man named Peter, a composer and Yale graduate who was looking for a sensitive and interesting woman to date. Linda and Peter agreed to meet at an outdoor Starbucks in the pretty Pacific Palisades near the beach. For the first hour, things went well, and conversation seemed easy and relaxed. Linda and Peter kind of hit it off.

But then an attractive blonde approached their table in an animated state. "Oh, my goodness, I can't believe it's you. Everything you predicted came true, even the fact that my husband was cheating on me! Of course, I divorced him."

Linda was shocked to have her secret of being a professional psychic exposed and felt very embarrassed. Then the woman turned to Linda's date, Peter. "Have you seen her and her sister on TV? They're incredible! How did you two meet?"

Peter looked increasingly uncomfortable as the woman, a client of ours, babbled on about our accuracy as psychics. He seemed to sink lower and lower into his chair as she talked, hiding behind his Foster Grants. Finally, Peter awkwardly rose from the table, extending his hand. "Linda, it's been a real pleasure meeting you," he said, sounding sincere. "You're a fabulous lady, really you are, but I just can't handle the fact that you are psychic. I'm so sorry, but I have to go."

With that, he left!

Linda's plan to keep the psychic thing a secret had backfired, and it was a hard lesson. After that, she resolved she would never try to conceal the fact again, even if it meant she would never have a second date. In fact, the very next date she went on, she greeted the guy with a sort of 12-step approach: " Hi, I'm Linda. I'm a psychic." To her great surprise, he said he was a psychic too!

Another guy Linda dated was a doctor in the health clinic that Terry managed. Robert was very self-impressed, and had published a book about a stress-free meditation program he developed. He was offering workshops in the Santa Monica area. On their second date, Linda discovered that Robert was a pot-head who needed to smoke dope to get through the day. No wonder he was stress free. If he needed drugs to relax, the claims that he made about his stress program were a bit dubious.

One rather large stumbling block is that all the men in L.A. are dating each other. Meanwhile, Terry dated an architect named Bill for a short while. Bill was a mountain bike fanatic who had ten racing bikes in his small studio apartment. A handsome guy with a perfectly chiseled body, Bill would show up on dates with gifts for Terry from Victoria's Secret: black satin thongs and pink lace bikini underwear. Terry was impressed until she discovered that Bill was wearing them himself! It didn't last long.

In springtime of 2004, we made our first trip to Paris and Amsterdam. Terry had broken up with a photographer named Jake several months earlier. While boarding the plane at LAX airport, Jake ambushed us and announced that he was taking the same flight to Paris. Terry was not totally shocked (psychic, you know), and she kept her composure, humoring him during the twelve-hour trip.

Linda's boyfriend at the time, David, was an Emmy-award winning TV set designer based in New York City. He met us at the DeGaulle airport, and he was amazed to see that Jake was trailing us. We quickly left Jake behind and the three of us went on to our hotel, then out for dinner. At midnight there was a knock on Terry's door. "It's Jake, I'm in the room next to yours."

Alarmed, Terry's mind raced. "I've gone to bed," she told him, not wanting to provoke him further. Terry was understandably terrified, and quickly phoned Linda and David. Thankfully, David kicked Jake out of the hotel the following morning. She never saw him again. It was not the first time that we had been stalked, but it was the most extreme case to date. Jake later sent a bill to Terry, tallying his expenses for the entire time they had dated each other, including a the cost of a new toilet he had installed in his apartment.

He was certainly a memory to flush away.

On returning to the States, Linda had a persistent funny feeling that David was seeing another woman in New York. When she confronted him about it, he lied at first, and then admitted sheepishly that there had been some other dates with a "gal pal" in recent weeks. Linda ended the relationship.

Rule #1: Don't ever try to fool a psychic.

It is not uncommon for men to be threatened by the close bond that twins share. Most of the identical twins we know have remained single well past their forties. We ourselves have had numerous boyfriends who could not handle the friendship we have. They felt compelled to compete with the close communication that we have established over a lifetime of being together. Men know when they meet us that we are a package deal. We both have to like him. Insecure guys find this intimidating.

One of Linda's stranger relationships was with an acupuncturist and healer in his late forties named Taylor. Taylor was an admitted recluse, and at the time was on a raw food diet, eating slabs of raw fish and whole bunches of bananas at a sitting. He was intrigued by our psychic abilities, and amazed by the level of psychic energy the two of us could manage at a given time. Linda was drawn to Taylor because he worked in healing and greatly respected her talents and esoteric interests.

She thought, what a relief to finally meet a man who isn't afraid of a strong woman.

But then came the red flags.

Taylor would meditate for hours every day, even forgetting to show up on dates because he had drifted too deep into trance. He lived only a few blocks away from Linda, but rarely came by. When he did, he wouldn't even knock; he left a business card. He insisted that he wanted to marry her, have a child with her and set up a healing center. However, Linda was skeptical, and Terry didn't trust him either.

Finally, he admitted that yes, in fact, he had lied about all of it.

Months after the breakup, Taylor wrote a letter saying, "I was heartbroken to find there was no chance for us. I must apologize for wasting your time and wasting my chances for a future with you while being obsessed with being enlightened. When indeed you are wed, please alert me so that I can string model airplanes across my ceiling as a tribute to prolonged adolescence."

Linda was crestfallen, wondering if she could ever find an honest, kind, and spiritual marriage partner in this life. Do all men misrepresent themselves in some way, she wondered? Judging from the hundreds of people we have read (and dated) over the years, the answer, unfortunately, is yes, many of them do. At best, it felt as though we were characters in an absurd situation comedy.

A few years later, we got a call from a producer who was interviewing for a new show. The show never happened, but Tom emailed Terry, saying that he wanted to take her to dinner. Terry wasn't attracted to him but she decided that one dinner seemed harmless enough. Tom showed up with his dog, and gushed over him like a mother with a new baby. On their date, Tom bragged about his shows, his two Emmy awards, his celebrity friends, and his extensive DVD collection. After dinner on their second date, Terry asked if he had ever been married. "Kinda sorta," Tom replied awkwardly. "I married a woman in Peru, but she dumped me."

Terry's psychic radar was on high alert.

"Did you get divorced in Peru?" she asked, half jokingly. Here was a guy whose type we call an "entrenched bachelor," because he is so terrified of commitment. "No," Tom replied simply, and dropped it. Over several weeks, he sent several effusive love letters to Terry, and in the last one admitted that he had two other girlfriends. When Terry realized that Tom approached dating like an audition--not that unusual in Tinseltown--she declined his ardent pleas to continue seeing her. She informed him that she was looking for a boyfriend, not a harem! We later discovered that he had spent two years in prison for running a house of prostitution, disguised as a healing retreat, in the upscale Hollywood Hills.

Do soulmates exist? Oh, definitely. But not in Hollywood. Dating is like shopping at Loehman's. You have to keep going back until they put the good stuff out on the rack.

Thank God we have a sense of humor.

Chapter Fifteen

THE OTHER SIDE

"The person who says it cannot be done should not interrupt the person who is doing it."

-Les Brown

We speak

Since our move to L.A., we began doing some readings for friends who were referring their friends to us. We began to get reports from our new clients that our predictions were accurate. The positive feedback increased our confidence, so we bravely decided to place a ten-dollar ad in *The Whole Earth Calendar*, a local newspaper.

Ten bucks was about all we could afford, due to all our ever-present medical bills. The ad was so small, you needed a magnifying glass to read it. About a week later, we received a call. It was a producer named Lori Weiss, calling from NBC's hit show *The Other Side*. This innovative talk show, hosted by Dr. Will Miller, focused on metaphysical subjects, the paranormal, ghosts, UFO's, holistic medicine, and unexplained phenomena. Lori had seen our ad, and she asked us if we were really twins. Linda assured her that we were in fact identical twins, probably the only psychic twins in the world. We have neither heard of, nor have we met other identical twins who work as we do. "Are you really psychic?" Lori challenged. "Yes," Linda responded. "We're clairvoyant and we predict the future using automatic writing." "Can you do a reading for me right now?" Lori asked. "Sure," Linda answered, swallowing hard. "You have ear infections... and a serious stomach illness."

Lori was dead silent for a moment. "You're exactly right. I have Krohn's disease. And ear infections. Keep going." Linda continued. "You've been through a recent breakup, which was very difficult for you. But I see you meeting someone very soon by the name of Steve." Lori confirmed the breakup. (She called us later that week to tell us she had met a guy named Steve at an expo. They had hit it off).

"Wow. That's the most accurate reading I've ever had!" Lori exclaimed after Linda finished. "Would you two be willing to appear on our show on Wednesday? The theme will be "intuitive diagnosis," and the show will feature four professional psychics who read illness in different ways.

You'll be diagnosing someone's illness psychically, and a reputable medical doctor will be there to verify your findings." Remember, Lori had not asked Linda to diagnose her illness. That just happened to be the first thing Linda picked up on.

She went on to say that Sylvia Browne, the most famous psychic medium, who has been a regular guest on *The Montel Williams Show*, and Suzanne Myles, then known as Australia's best psychic, would be on the panel with us.

We couldn't believe this was happening.

Linda quickly agreed, hung up the phone and screamed. "We're going to be on NBC!" Terry joined her, jumping around the room. It had never occurred to us that we would appear as psychics on national television. Most psychics spend years and big bucks promoting themselves to get this chance. We sensed that this was one of those divinely orchestrated opportunities to expand our abilities and franchise our frequency.

And just like *Saturday Night Live*, it dropped into our laps seemingly out of the blue. *The Other Side* was so new, we had not even seen it ourselves. It was an hour-long talk show that aired at 9:00 a.m. daily (Los Angeles time). Fortunately, we had both recently quit our day jobs as secretaries (yay!). Deepak

Chopra and medium James Van Praagh were frequent guests on the show. We were excited, yet terrified. Having had precious little experience diagnosing illnesses in other people, this was a huge risk. We could wind up looking really bad if we misdiagnosed. We prayed to be protected, and trusted our spirit guides to be there for us. It felt exactly as if we were leaping off a steep cliff without a net to catch us. How many times had we taken daredevil risks like this before? Countless times. Our personal philosophy had always been to say yes to everything. (We say no to a lot of things now.) That credo has paid off for us.

We were able to gain valuable experience in many areas by jumping in and doing things we were afraid to do. There is no turning back now, we thought as we entered the doors of NBC studios. Lori greeted us at the door of the Green room with contracts in hand. Several nervous-looking guests sat in stony silence on leather couches, barely touching the Kraft service food. These were the people we would be reading on camera, and we were quickly segregated from them. Medium James Van Praagh was on the TV monitor, finishing the taping of a segment about mediumship. The energy of the room powerfully shifted when he walked into the room, chatting and joking with Terry as he reached for the phone. We exchanged business cards, feeling more relaxed now. Terry, of course, was developing a throbbing migraine headache. Psychic Sylvia Browne bustled into the room with her husband.

"Who's got the migraine? " she exclaimed. "I know it's not mine--my head is splitting!" We laughed and Terry owned up that the headache was hers. Somehow, she got through the ordeal with grace and courage. The angels were with us, and miraculously we were swept onstage with this formidable panel of mystics. Host Dr. Will Miller entered the stage. He has several degrees in theology and psychology. Like us, he had been a professional comic in New York at one time. A tall, slim man in his late forties, with silver hair and wire-rimmed glasses, Will put us at ease with his warm and affable manner. We liked him immediately. The medical expert was Dr. Susan Hufnagel, a controversial Los Angeles gynecologist. She was clearly anti-psychic and rather belligerent towards the psychics present. Several of Dr. Hufnagel's patients sat next to us. We were asked to divine one woman's illness. She appeared to be about forty, with short brown hair and a pullover sweater, and sat smiling primly with her hands folded on her lap. She was as closed as her doctor. "What can you tell us about Donna?" Will Miller prompted us. We began writing.

"Donna has a significant block of energy in the colon and uterus," we said. "She has a lot of fear about her illness." We also stated that we picked up on allergies. We had hit a bulls-eye. There was a hush in the audience as Sylvia leaned over and gave us a thumb's up. Words can't express how relieved we were when Dr. Hufnagel conceded that Donna did, in fact, have a large uterine tumor, as well as serious allergies. The guides were with us!

A friend of ours named Lou Martin was in the audience watching the segment.
A well-known channeler himself, Lou has the ability to see auras as well. He commented that while we were onstage, a brilliant gold light surrounded us and he could see lightning shooting out of our fingertips while we did our automatic writing. Many psychics have told us that during lectures we appear as though we are standing in columns of gold light.

After the show aired, we received hundreds of phone calls from all over the country, and were asked to appear two more times on *The Other Side*.

NBC had launched our new career as professional psychics.

Chapter Sixteen

CONNECTING THE COSMIC DOTS

"Intuition is really a sudden immersion of the soul into the universal current of life, where the histories of all people are connected, and we are able to know everything, because it's all written there."

- Paul Coelho

We encourage anyone who is wanting a reading to keep an open mind. People who are skeptical or fearful about getting a psychic reading tend to suck all the air out of the room like a black hole, making information more difficult to receive. It helps when the sitter is in a space of openness to allow the free flow and exchange of energy. This will maximize the effectiveness of the reading. We often tell our clients that the clearer they are about their questions, the clearer the answers will be from the spirit realm. Meditating before your psychic session can be of great benefit.

Often someone is quite cut off, or emotionally blocked, and out of touch with his or her feelings. This makes us and the spirit world work twice as hard. Our friend Maggie used to say, "Testing a psychic is like teaching a pig to sing. It's a waste of time and it annoys the pig!" It detracts from the quality of the result. One would do better to choose a psychic with a proven track record and documented proof of their predictions (either in print, television, or radio recording).

Sometimes we will decline to read a person a second time if we feel they are deliberately testing us, arguing with the information we receive, or somehow blocking the energy. Men have a tendency to do this more than women, because women are naturally more in touch with their intuition. Some people, during an in-person reading, will sit and stare at us like zombies, as if they are watching us on TV. Then, at the end of the session, they suddenly have a miliion questions for us. It is almost as if they need an hour or so to get used to our energy.

Skeptics have called us and said "I've been disappointed in psychics in the past, but I trust you two completely. You seem so sincere." Some have followed our career for literally years before calling us for a private session. More than one client has had a dream about psychic twins, subsequently searched the Internet for our website and showed up at our door, without quite knowing why!

There are those who won't listen or take any advice to achieve their dreams, but then make the psychic wrong or somehow to blame for their failure. This is commonplace in our field of work. Psychics cannot live your life for you. Will Rogers said, "Even if you're on the right track, you'll get run over if you just sit there!" We are psychics, not magicians. Your destiny is in your hands, not in ours, and only you have the power to create your future.

We recently read an article in the L.A. Times about psychics in Russia. It was not really surprising to learn that when the Russian police fail to solve a criminal case, they blame the psychics in town. This is tantamount to kicking your cat if you have had a bad day. Intuitive counselors are conduits for guidance and inspiration, and you must take the initiative to make your dreams happen. At any point in time there are a number of probable events or outcomes that can result from the action one takes, or does not take. We take a "snapshot" of the most probable or likely outcome based on subtle energies that we interpret in the sitter's electromagnetic field, as well as the information that we receive through our automatic writing process. Everyone has free will to influence an outcome. We teach people to live "at cause" rather than "at effect" in their daily lives, giving them real tools for growth and change.

Although some have called us "sentient computers," psychics are not computers. Don't expect a psychic to solve all your problems in twenty minutes, or to know every single obstacle you will confront, including names and dates. We have a friend in England, a professional psychic, who calls these "McDonald's Readings." In other words, we are so accustomed to fast food that we think we should solve our problems just as quickly--or rather, we think that the psychics should! One woman, a reputable author, came to us for a reading. She later told her friend that she was upset that we didn't tell her she was pregnant. Our response was, "You didn't ask!"

To give another example, we once warned a client about his car. We told him we felt it was dangerous to drive, and warned him strongly about keeping it. He didn't pay attention, and took the car on a road trip that same weekend. It broke down in East Podunk, Idaho, in the middle of the night. It took him all night to get a tow truck, and he finally got home at five o'clock in the morning. This guy called us and chastised us for not insisting that he sell it! We explained to him that he had not wanted to hear what we were saying, and it was an obvious lesson that he needed to learn. We are messengers... don't shoot the messenger! What you do with the information is up to you.

No psychic should ever tell you what to do, or control you. Some psychics do this, and it is to their own detriment. Our job is to guide you in making the best decisions based on assistance from your angels and guides as well as ours. We take great pride in our work, and treat each person with extreme care, whether we are doing a short reading or a long one. It is almost like a spiritual "research process." As we mentioned, we access the Akasha, a sort of "cosmic library." In our twenty-plus years in the metaphysical field, we have developed a divination system that is quite unique.

Every psychic person works differently, in his or her own way. Some use psychometry (the ability to receive impressions by touching objects related to someone), others use tarot cards or runes, some interpret dreams, others choose not to use tools of any particular kind. Very few psychics use the technique of automatic writing, and we have developed our own method into a virtual science. We are all interpreting messages or impressions at a subliminal level. Unlike other psychics who occasionally receive "a bolt from the blue" about a future occurrence, the sensations we are interpreting are often much more subtle and impressionistic than this. For us, we are reliably psychic for anyone, anywhere, anytime. It is like turning on a radio. This does not mean that we always can be "on," or that we would even want to be computer-like. No psychic living is 100% accurate, although some may claim to be. We are human beings. Diligent practice is the only way to learn to discern between one's subconscious feelings and information coming from another source. We feel a big part of our purpose is to create a bridge of understanding so that we can all embrace our intuitive gifts without fear.

Chapter Seventeen

DOUBLE VISIONARIES

"The greatest thing a human being ever does in this world is to see something. To see clearly is poetry, prophecy and religion, all in one."

— *John Ruskin*

We have been working in the metaphysical field as professional psychics for over twenty years, using the unusual form of divination previously touched on known as "automatic writing" or "channeled writing." We connect with other forms of intelligence, tapping into a broader knowing. Automatic writing is considered to be the only way one can access the "Akashic Records," or the "Akasha," which is an etheric band surrounding the planet that contains a record of all thought and deed (not to be confused with the "other side" or the sleeping place of spirits). Our actions and thoughts do not simply disappear, but are recorded in the ethers of the universe, which is the Akasha.

Automatic writing is a vehicle by which we bring in specific messages or information about the past lives or future of an individual. We have broadened it to include world prophecy, for which we are best known. Some of the world predictions we have made in national magazines or on public radio include:

9/11 World Trade Center terrorist attacks
May 2000 Stock Market Crash
George W. Bush Presidential win in 2000
George W. Bush Re-election in 2004
The War in Afghanistan

The War in Iraq
The Florida Hurricanes in 2004
Earthquakes in Mexico and Japan in 2004
JFK Jr.'s death in a small plane
Names and location of Maryland snipers
Conviction of Scott Peterson (and location of Laci's body)

When we do a psychic reading with someone, we do not need to be sitting in person with that individual. Since we are accessing information fields, we can read for people all over the world. All we need is a person's name, and we start writing even before the person calls us, obtaining information about their past, present and future. Our hands move across the paper without our conscious direction, as if an unseen entity is guiding them. We are in what is called a "conscious trance," so we can let our mind move aside, as it were, in order to discern the spirit communication. We were never taught how to do this, nor have we known anyone else who works this way. That is because we are "spirit-taught," which means we received all of our instruction directly from our angels and spirit guides. Perfecting it took us many years of daily practice.

When we first started writing nearly twenty years ago, we discovered that we could channel pages and pages of detailed information on subjects about which we consciously knew nothing. Even more surprising is that as twins, we can be in two different rooms and channel almost identical information. We are known as a "bifurcated soul," or one soul with two bodies. This is very unusual for twins. Our extraordinary intuitive gifts come from a combination of factors. As artists, we feel that art is a form of channeling. We have always been spiritual seekers, which is why started practicing Buddhism twenty years ago. Chanting and meditating many hours a day really opened up our psychic abilities to a great extent.

To receive a message from the guides is a very strange, magical phenomenon. We ask a question of our guides and of the guides of the person we're reading. We receive a block of thought, interpret it, and write it simultaneously. This is a form of claircognizance, or clear knowing. This process was frightening for us at first; many people in our culture are threatened by their innate psychic gifts, mostly due to a lack of information and understanding. At first we doubted the information we received, questioning its validity. When reading for others, we are shouldering a tremendous amount of responsibility for his or her life course. To bolster our confidence, we would compare our answers with each other, testing ourselves for accuracy on a constant basis. We hold ourselves to a high degree of integrity, and at first we felt we needed to "know everything," like a sentient computer. We later learned that no psychic could possibly do this, and that other psychics are very vague in their information. We have been told we are much more detailed and more accurate than other psychics, who are often reading a reflection of the Akasha, and thereby receiving a distortion of the truth.

When we do readings, we receive specific messages, names, dates, times, descriptions and information about past lives, present, and future. We get a lot of numbers which we interpret as days, months, or years. A handwriting expert once told us that our writing is like a "violin melody, so fine, loose, and sensitive—like a dance into other spheres of existence."

We do believe that as humans we can know the unknowable (although not everything), and that the power of the mind and spirit is boundless. We believe it is our mission to use our gifts to create a bridge between earth and the unseen realms of spirit. Psychic work allows us to see past illusion to what is real.

In over twenty years of work in the metaphysical field, we have assisted police in murder investigations, reunited people with their birth families and predicted key events for the millennium. While many twins are known to have heightened intuition with each other, we can reliably predict the future for other people.

Andrei Ridgeway comments that "the seer is not just a holy person, but also a realist. Using a fine balance of spiritual insight and common sense, the seer makes predictions that take into account the laws of probability and change." What we do is more of an art than it is a science. This is why we feel that psychics do not always respond well to testing.

Some say the role of the prophet is to show what could be, so that we may make changes in the present to prevent unfavorable events from manifesting. At any point in time, there are a number of probable events that may occur, depending on one's karmic "blueprint" and the choices we make moment by moment. As psychics, we help people to become aware of possible roadblocks ahead and give them tools for expanding their awareness and changing their destiny. We feel that each soul's lesson and opportunity lies within whatever struggle may be at hand. The story *The Wizard of Oz* by L. Frank Baum is a spiritual one about a young girl getting past obstacles to align with her authentically empowered self. Dorothy discovers on her journey that she must look within herself to truly "go home," and finds that ability has been inside her all along. Our goal and intention as psychics is to put people on track with their purpose in life, to help them look inside to find their own personal yellow brick road, as we did.

Chapter Eighteen

TWINSIGHT

"There are things known and there are things unknown, and in between are the doors of perception."

--Aldous Huxley

One of the psychic gifts we have developed over the years is the ability to discern, describe, and diagnose illness in others. This is known as "medical intuitive" work, a term popularized by author Carolyn Myss. We "read" the energy fields within and around the body, picking up specific information about energy blocks and imbalances that may be useful in enhancing a person's health and well-being. We jokingly say that we have this unique ability due to having suffered so many illnesses ourselves! But a lifetime of seeking out alternative therapies and calling on our psychic guides helped us to hone an innate intuitive talent.

Years ago, early in our career, we did a reading for a pretty young 28-year-old woman we'll call "Jenna." She was the picture of health, blonde with pink rosy cheeks and a bubbly personality. As we tuned in and began scanning her body, we were both surprised to find ourselves writing that she in fact would be dealing with breast cancer within a short period of time. Jenna was in disbelief when we told her this, because she was so young and had no family history of cancer. She had also recently changed her career course and was starting college classes to become a physician's assistant. Fortunately, Jenna took the prediction seriously and decided to go for a mammogram to see if we were right. Sure enough, she was diagnosed with 4th stage breast cancer, and underwent a radical mastectomy. She later called to thank us, saying that if we had not warned her about the cancer, she never would have gotten a checkup, and most likely would have died.

We once told a nice lady we'll call "Margie" that she should have her gynecologist check her for ovarian cysts. She went for a check-up, and her doctor pronounced her to be healthy. She immediately protested, "No, there are cysts—you must check again." When he asked how she knew this to be true, she said, "The Psychic Twins told me. Please check again!" Her gynecologist eyed her with suspicion and said, "You're an intelligent woman—I am surprised that you believe in that psychic nonsense." Margie convinced him to re-examine her-- this time with an ultrasound device-- and to his astonishment, found that we were absolutely right. He had overlooked her ovarian cysts and she had surgery soon after—just in time!

Another client "Dani" arrived for a consultation, and was visibly distraught. Using our automatic writing, we quickly determined that she had a rare form of cancer, and had recently undergone surgery. "You are right, I have a rare liposarcoma (cancer), and I had one of my kidneys removed, but the doctors gave me only a few months to live." Dani started to cry. "My friends can't believe this is happening to me."

We tuned into her etheric body, and felt strongly that she would defy the odds and go into remission. We did some energy healing on Dani, and urged her to do daily visualization, to see the tumor bathed alternately in green and violet healing light. By focusing on the healing and dissolving of the cancer, she would have a strong chance of overcoming this difficult illness. "Focus on what you want to see happen, instead of what you are afraid of happening," we told her. "It will require pulling something powerful out of you life, really developing your faith."

"But the statistics are not in my favor," Dani protested.

"Don't buy into the statistics. We see a clean bill of health by June, and we don't see another surgery," Terry said firmly. We coached her not to pay attention to the negativity and fear of those around her, passively accepting a bleak prognosis.

"Just because your doctors and friends are negative," Linda told her," it doesn't mean you can't create a miracle." We counseled her on many different techniques, meditations, and dietary changes that could support her healing, as well as creative tools such as painting and journal writing.

Two months later, we heard from a friend of Dani's that her cancer had gone into total remission, shocking all the doctors! We live in a society where it is easy to find agreement about the hopelessness of illness, especially cancer. It is crucial that we challenge our deeply ingrained beliefs about what is possible, to demonstrate amazing and miraculous results in our lives. We are all capable of so much more than we have been taught to believe. Illness demands that one begin to look within, to develop new habits of thought and action. It requires of us to develop a new kind of consciousness.

Forgiveness and self-love are extremely important in the healing process. Achieving this may be more difficult than we think. But we can begin by asking "what is the lesson here for me?" Often illness holds a spiritual teaching for us, or shines a light on an emotion we have held for too long, such as anger or grief. Sometimes it can be helpful to release old feelings through a ritual such as burning letters or photographs that are holding us to the past. "Spirit, I am now free. I do not need these feelings anymore."

Infertility is so devastating, so it is not surprising that we get a lot of people desiring counseling on this topic. One week, we received five calls from women whose babies we predicted! The most dramatic story was a young woman we'll call "Carrie."

Carrie was our dental hygienist, a delightful and angelic girl of twenty-one. When she married a young dentist, we coached her through those first difficult years. The problem was that she could not get pregnant, no matter what she tried. We had seen her having children, and predicted that she would conceive within two to three years, and get pregnant with a girl, then a boy. We advised her to improve her diet, to learn to manage the stress in her life, and to work through some of the painful abuse she had suffered in childhood. Carrie underwent several in-vitro fertility treatments with no success. She resisted addressing her diet and emotional issues, not really seeing these as having any connection to her infertility.

When she came to us after a couple of years in utter frustration, we told her we still saw a pregnancy against all odds by the following October, but she had to follow strict ground rules: her diet *had* to change, and she had to start taking better care of herself. We referred her to an excellent prenatal nutritionist, and she promised this time to do what we advised. After another year, she and her husband arrived to see us, with their new baby boy! It turned out that the girl we saw her having was in fact her first pregnancy a year earlier, which had ended in a miscarriage. And she finally became pregnant that October, just as we had said. Little Josh was a real "miracle" baby.

Another young mother, a neighbor in our building, by chance ran into Linda on her way to the doctor. She was very upset about her new baby's health. Dmitri was suffering from unexplained stomach problems, and was unable to keep anything down for months. Mom Sasha was also suffering from severe gall bladder pain since giving birth. Linda tuned in and told her that Dmitri would be fine, with a slightly modified diet. When Sasha said her doctor feared she herself would have to have gall bladder surgery within the week, Linda had a sudden strong sense that surgery would be unnecessary, and even harmful for her. She shared her feeling with Sasha, but encouraged her to follow her doctor's guidance. As psychics, we are very careful not to control people. Some psychics can be extremely controlling, insisting that you do as they say. (You would do well to avoid this type of intuitive counselor.) To Linda's surprise, Sasha decided to cancel her apppointment with the doctor that day. Instead, she took her baby, her mother and grandmother and went to a local hot springs for the weekend. Linda did not know Sasha trusted her as much as she did. She was shocked when Sasha told her. As it turned out, both mother and baby were perfectly healthy within a couple of weeks. No surgeries were necessary, and today they are both thriving and happy. In fact, at age one and a half, little Dmitri seems to have superhuman strength, and his parents are considering putting him in Olympic training as soon as he is old enough!

Much has been written about twin telepathy, and we experience it on a daily basis. There are many stories of twins feeling each other's pain, and even of one twin experiencing her twin sister's labor pains! We spend so much time together that we almost don't need to speak to each other to know the other's thoughts. We "read each other's minds" all day long, and have always had identical illnesses. The most powerful example of this, along the lines of medical intuition, probably saved Terry's life.

Terry once went on a date with a guy that involved hiking up a small mountain. It was a gorgeous sunny day, but she was coming down with a cold and decided to challenge herself in spite of it. By the time she got home, she was feeling very ill, and tumbled into bed. Over the next few hours, she lost her voice, her eyes swelled up, she lost her hearing, and was struggling to breathe. She was too sick to get out of bed, so she sent a mental cry for help to Linda, who was out with her boyfriend David at the time. Linda must have received the telepathic message, because while on the date she suddenly got the strongest urge to get home. Something was definitely very wrong. David protested, but Linda was insistent, and she arrived home just in time to get Terry to the hospital emergency room. Terry had a severe case of a flu virus, and Linda had reached her at the crucial moment. Another hour may have been too late.

Chapter Nineteen

SYDNEY FINDS HER BIRTH FAMILY

"What would our day look like if we saw in infrared and ultraviolet, or if we could train ourselves to see auras, futures unformed, pasts lingering?"

- Richard Bach

Our intuitive consultations have reunited loved ones, saved marriages, prevented suicides, and led people to the right healing tools. One of the most dramatic reunion stories involved a beautiful young woman we'll call "Sydney."

Sydney looked like a model, with striking long red hair and refined features. Right away, we picked up that Sydney was adopted as a baby. Although she loved her adoptive parents, she was in deep pain. Her mother had passed away, and she desperately wanted to find her "birth parents." Using automatic writing, we told her that she would find them within three weeks in Canada, and, moreover, that they were looking for her! She was amazed and encouraged. Although at the time we knew very little about the internet, Sydney's spirit guides were clearly encouraging her to use that method for her search. We gave her the names and detailed descriptions of her long-lost family members, including her mother, a brother and sister, and her sister's baby.

Within three weeks, Sydney called us, incredulous. Her voice was filled with excitement. Everything had transpired as we had predicted. Even the names and details of her relatives matched. And she had found them on the internet, in Canada as we had seen. She was eagerly making plans to fly to Canada to meet with them. Since that time, they have visited one another and Sydney has become closer to her birth mom. She sometimes brings us photos and shares tapes of our sessions with her "new" family. We wish all adoptees could have this much success. It is heartwarming to know that we could help to facilitate this joyous family reunion.

Chapter Twenty

MEDIUMS RARE

"Ever since Stan died, we hardly ever see him anymore."

- Karen, in "Will and Grace"

We speak

In addition to accessing information fields, we also work as radio receivers through which spirits communicate. This is known as mediumship. While we cannot control who may come in with a message or how long the spirit may stay, we have been successful in bringing in messages from thousands of deceased people. Often we will receive specific names, personal details, and even how the person passed. When we both write the same names, we know it is probably a significant personal relationship to the sitter. In instances where we might mention a name and the sitter does not recognize it, we ask them to write it down, as often they will find later on in talking with family members that it is, in fact, the name of an aunt, cousin, acquaintance, or family member who has passed. We always get the phone call later: "My God, Esther is my mother-- what was I thinking?" Often, the spirit will speak in the tone or personality that he or she had while living, either expressing a humorous, mischievous, or loving energy that the communicator possessed in physical incarnation.

Communication with discarnate beings has been practiced for centuries, though always amid great controversy. This phenomenon has in recent years become widely accepted--if little understood--by modern society, largely due to popular TV shows such as *Medium* and *Crossing Over*. It is refreshing to see a growing open-mindedness that did not exist even five years ago. Public interest in mediumship has grown since the mid-19th century. It is a fact that President Lincoln and his wife, Mary Todd Lincoln, held seances in the White House in attempts to contact their son Willie. He had contracted typhoid in 1862, and died at the age of 12. Some researchers claim that the President and his wife actually had a sixteen-year-old psychic medium move into the White House to live with them.

Thomas Edison, the inventor, is documented in *Scientific American* as saying, "I do claim that it is possible to construct an apparatus which will be so delicate that if there are personalities in another existence or sphere who wish to get in touch with us... this apparatus will at least give them a better opportunity." Edison was developing this machine in the years just prior to his death, but he died before it was perfected. There is now a science specifically devoted to this exploration called Electronic Voice Phenomena, or EVP. It is also known as Instrumental Transcommunication, or ITC.

People have asked us if psychic work and mediumship is scary for us. We have not really been afraid of it, except in certain instances where we were asked to work on high-profile murder cases, and then we became concerned that we ourselves might become targets. If anything, we are fascinated by the powers of the "sixth sense." When we sit down to do a reading, we often have a sense of excitement that wells up. It feels as though beings are gathering around to help us give the person we are reading a gift that could be life-changing, pivotal in some way. Dependiing on the openness of that person to receive "the gift," the information can shift something on a deep level for his or her soul's life path.

Mediumship is not the same thing as clairvoyance. Not all

psychics are mediums. And contrary to popular belief, not all mediums are psychic (that is, have the gift of predicting the future). Every psychic or medium has a different style of working, using different strengths. Many psychics can read the energy field or "aura" of a person but cannot connect with spirits who have crossed over to the heavenly realms. We do both psychic work and mediumship. For many years we have been practicing a form of mediumship that our guides taught us through our automatic writing. Often the loved one's messages and thoughts comes through in the form of a letter. We have often wondered what it would be like to do mediumship without the writing. We spent years searching for the right teacher, even to the point of asking successful mediums to teach us the techniques, but no one wanted to teach it. Back in the 70's and 80's, it was impossible to find good psychics who would teach either discipline. Now it is more common, although we feel good psychics are as hard to find as good doctors. (Don't get us started on that one.)

Many mediums work according to a kind of "formula" or a structure that involves interpreting symbols and their meanings. For example, a vision of a birthday cake means there is a birthday coming soon, a rose means someone is sending love from the other side. Other television mediums have similar things in common with their approaches, though their personalities are very different. We have never worked as they do, using traditional symbols. Later we will explain to you why this is actually beneficial. But as we began to work with other mediums we became more curious about the background and tradition of this art form we were using, and wanted to study it. Our chance finally came. Chris, a nurse from Oregon, came in with her son to get readings. We hit it off like we'd known each other for eons, and out of the blue she said, "You two have to come up to Seattle for the mediumship seminar. It's being led by two famous British mediums from Arthur Findlay College in Stanstead. I feel that you are supposed to be there. In fact I'm sure of it. You can stay with my friends and rent their extra room for the week."

Without missing a beat, we agreed to sign up. It was one of those things you know you don't have to think about because if feels so right. This was true synchronicity operating, or as we say in Buddhism, "we were in rhythm with the Universe." It was by divine design.

We made all the travel arrangements, and everything fell into place easily. We got a great deal on the flights, her friends rented us the extra condo for an incredibly low rate, and Chris made plans to pick us up at the airport. We would spend an entire week in an intensive workshop called "Aspects of Mediumship."

On a chilly Seattle morning in September, we attended the seminar with about fourteen others. Everyone was so pleasant, despite being a bit nervous in anticipation of the mystical experiences to come. We sat around conversing, our chairs arranged in a circle, when the teachers entered. Nora Shaw, who is one of the best mediums in England, could be a twin to our mother. We liked her instantly. A petite woman in her 70's, she seemed tireless in her love of sharing her knowledge of spiritualism with us. Using great wit, her blue eyes would sparkle as she began to talk about the history of the "art" of mediumship. Her partner, Dr. Ann Marshall, was a stout woman with short black hair and twinkly blue eyes, who was not only a medium but a podiatrist and hypnotherapist. Ann sat beside Nora in almost total silence for quite awhile, closely listening, watching, observing. Later she opened up and entertained us with her dry humor. Both of them demonstrated their own special gifts that day, but we didn't expect what happened next.

Nora began to speak. "I have here a lady who looks a great

deal like me, and she is with another woman who resembles her who has Alzheimer's."

"Nora, that is our grandmother," Terry said. "And our Mom has a condition of dementia that the doctors think may be Alzheimer's. Could it be them? Our Mom is still living."

Nora replied, "Often people with Alzheimer's are doing a lot of work with the spirit world in preparation to leave the Earth plane. Your grandmother is helping your mother to make the transition from Earth to the astral realm."

Tears began streaming down our faces. Nana died when we were only three years old, but we remember her as being a warm and loving person who truly cared about us. It felt somewhat magical, yet comforting at the same time, to connect with her energy after all these years.

Ann added, "Your grandmother was very psychic, but she couldn't talk about it in her day." People often ask us if psychics run in our family. "No, we tend to walk a lot," is our response! But seriously, if our relatives were psychic, it certainly had never been revealed to any of us-- that is, until that day.

We worked in groups from early morning until six o'clock at night, practicing techniques designed to "attune" us to a higher sensitivity and vibration. Terry cried a great deal, healing the grief that she had held onto for so long. There was such extraordinary healing energy present. The two of us knew we were releasing emotions of shock and sadness that we had been long suppressing from the loss of Conner... 9/11... and all the years of illness and struggle and poverty. It was transformational and we will always remember it. We wrote, we shared stories, we laughed, we took turns reading each other alone and in groups. There were meditations to music and we even colored with crayons to help us attune even more to our higher guidance.

By the third day we were all feeling a bit more comfortable. The two of us had not been sleeping well. We entered the classroom to find over forty people, who had come in for only one day of the seminar. Ann announced, "I need a volunteer...TERRY!" and stared directly at Terry as she said it. Terry's heart was in her throat. She stood alone before the group, wondering if she could do this "off book," that is, without clutching her trusty pad and pen. It was unnerving, but she often thinks of the Nike ad "Just do it!" in situations like this and she just..well, did it.

"A woman is presenting herself to me who is tall," Terry began, "With dark red curls piled on top of her head, and big blue eyes. Her gown is very glamorous and it is made of gold silk. She is holding a wooden inlaid box and offering it as a gift. She is giving me the names Patricia and Theresa." Suddenly, Terry was embodying the woman's spirit. Amazingly, the information kept coming, and she just went with it, trusting it. At times she would raise her arm to write in the air out of habit, and sort of like Dr. Strangelove she would have to use her other arm to push it down. Ann jokingly got Terry in a bear hug to break her of the habit of having to write while connecting with the spirit world. It worked. "She passed of a heart attack," Terry continued. "She loved dancing. 'I'm a very good dancer,' she is telling me. She is thanking you for all that you did for her." On and on and on.

Ann was writing everything down furiously on a large notepad behind me with a magic marker. After twenty minutes of this, Ann said to Terry, "Who is this woman wanting to speak to?" Terry walked straight ahead and gestured boldly to a woman in the chair before her, someone who she had never seen before in her life.

"Yes, that's my mother," the woman whispered. "My name is Patricia and my sister is Theresa. My mom looked just like that, and she used to wear her hair up... and she died of a heart attack. She was a professional dancer. Everything you said is true." Tears rolled down her face. A hush fell over the group, no one made a sound for several minutes afterward. Finally, Nora spoke. "That's very good, very good indeed. This is the kind of evidence that we need to show scientists who challenge the work of mediumship, because it proves how accurate it is. There is no way you could make this up, or know any of it. Excellent." Terry turned around, and on the board Ann was writing on were no fewer than thirty facts about the "spirit woman" she brought through that day, and every detail was accurate.

Psychic and mediumship work is still a relatively unexplored frontier, and we are proud to be helping to pioneer in the field for generations to come.

CONNER IN CYBERSPACE

"You might wake up some mornin'
To the sound of something moving past your
window in the wind.
You may see the floating motion of a distant
pair of wings...
Across my dreams with nets of wonder
I chase the bright elusive butterfly of love."

- "Elusive Butterfly" by Bob Lind

We speak

We had just returned from a lively party in the Hollywood Hills on a warm August night in 2000, when we received a call from our friend Steven.

"Conner killed himself last night."

Conner Berkeley (we have changed his name) had come to see us for a consultation several years before, and many times after that. We had become good friends. He was a vibrant, athletic young man in his early twenties who was embarking on a career in acting. His energy was so over-the-top that it was definitely suspect, yet his exuberance inspired everyone who met him. Conner was truly one of the funniest people we have ever met, often taking his humor to the extreme. We would learn that he had a long history of mental depression and that medication and therapy had been ineffective in treating his bipolar disorder. Since his teens, he had tried to commit suicide many times. We spent many hours encouraging him, and introduced him to the basic practice of Buddhism, which he embraced wholeheartedly. It enhanced his life, although it could not ultimately save him.

His death hit us both very hard, in fact we were inconsolable for weeks afterward. He had truly believed in us and he used to tell us "I'm going to the top and I'm taking you with me." At one point we were all up to star in a sitcom together for FOX, which wasn't meant to be. His career was not going as he planned, but he landed a supporting role opposite Michael Bolton in his feature film and seemed to be on an upswing in his life. We were all excited for him, and he was even dating someone new. But his inner demons got the best of him. After a bad breakup, he decided he couldn't take the pain anymore. He hanged himself in his apartment that fateful August night.

Anyone who has lost a loved one to suicide--friend or family member--knows that it is probably the most difficult thing that one can experience in a lifetime. There is the long grieving process and even more difficult, the anger, questioning, self-blame, and the sheer horror of the loss. Could we have done something more? Why did he do it? If only he had done this or that, given it more time to work the problem through. There are endless questions that never get answered. There is nothing one can do to save a manic depressive when that person is determined to take his or her own life.

In Buddhism, we had been taught that suicide solves nothing, and one's spirit must be reborn in order to repeat the lessons in the next life until the lessons are learned. Suicide is ultimately a selfish choice, because so many loved ones are left in pain and suffering. But we have come to understand that Conner made the decision in a moment of utter despair. Perhaps there truly was no other choice apparent to him in that moment. Because of our own battle with depression throughout our lives, we could understand and forgive it more easily than perhaps someone who has not been there. If you have thoughts of suicide, please seek professional help now, don't wait another day. You cannot imagine the pain your loved ones will carry if you make that choice.

Since his passing we have not only contacted Conner through automatic writing, he has visited us. The day that he died, while we were on our daily walk, a butterfly circled Linda and alighted on her heart (butterflies symbolize joy). He has since made his presence known by blinking lights on and off, turning on our car light, and writing us e-mails. Even the famous medium, John Edward, claims that this has happened to people that he knows. Spirits use electricity and other means of energy to get their message across, in whatever way possible, and that includes computers!

For a while every day, Conner would come through to us. We'd open up our e-mails for the day and they would be all jumbled and out of order. The eulogy that we had given at his funeral would pop up on the screen, or a significant excerpt, usually a Buddhist quote or guidance that a senior in faith had given us regarding his sudden death. That's how we knew it was Conner. We believe he would go into our hard drive and find the documents pertaining to him and send them to our email address! This was uncanny, yet it did happen. During a mediumship seminar in Seattle, the British medium Nora Shaw brought Conner through. She described him and the means by which he had passed. Through Nora, Conner told us, "I knew I'd made a mistake as soon as I did it. I regret it now. I love you both." It was a touching moment.

Occasionally something strange will happen and we'll look at each other and say in unison "It's Conner." Even in spirit, he is more alive than many who are living. We miss you, dear friend, and we know that one day you'll find the happiness you are seeking.

Chapter Twenty-One

THE DEATH BOAT

"I'm not afraid of death, I just don't want to be there when it happens."

-Woody Allen

We speak

We're fielding questions and making predictions to a group of 100 people. It could have been any lecture anywhere in the country, but this one was different. We are on The Norwegian Sky, one of the largest cruise ships in the world, and we're billed alongside of some of the most famous psychic mediums in the country. We set sail in the cobalt Caribbean, bound for Puerto Rico. The roster read like a Who's Who of mediums: nationally known Suzanne Northrup, rising stars John Holland and Lysa Mateu, angel channel Terra Sonora, psychic and author Barbara Stabiner, grief therapist Edie Nathan, and of course The Psychic Twins. For an entire week, we gave seminars, workshops and psychic readings for a ship full of people, many of whom were "dying" to connect with lost loved ones on the other side. Because for several years our primary focus had been television, this was a new and daunting experience for us. We had been wanting and waiting for the right opportunity to expand into lecturing, in order to broaden our horizons and our exposure. When Andrea and Janice contacted us about joining their "Intuvision Healing Cruise," we immediately signed on. One couldn't find a broader horizon than the Atlantic ocean! The Norwegian Sky was so huge, it reminded us of the Titanic. As we waited in line to board, we took in the majestic ship, its walls gleaming white like a huge skyscraper mirrored in the bluest of blue water. With some 2000 passengers and almost as many crew, this was some boat ride! Finally reaching our tiny room, we hastily unpacked our matching outfits and returned to deck for a safety run, which is kind of like a fire drill with life jackets. As the only twins on board, we stuck out like two sore thumbs in the crowd, and many people stopped to talk to us. Because of all the psychics present, everyone was jovial, and there was a circus atmosphere onboard. People sensed something special was about to happen. Grandparents proudly pulled out snapshots of the kids and grandkids to show us, others promised to schedule readings. By the end of the day our schedule was booked full.

"I wish I could clone you, so many people want to get readings with you!" Andrea exclaimed excitedly. "I could book you for a year!" "Too late for that, we are already cloned!" Terry quipped. We hurried from classroom to classroom, then ran back to our room for our private sessions with clients. There was barely enough time to eat. We spent what little spare time we had squeezing into group seances with the other mediums. There was much healing, and a lot of grief being released during this emotional week. At dinner time we all met in the main dining room, mingling with the guests and offering free readings over gourmet food. When we finally did eat, we ate well: filet mignon, lobster tail, chocolate mousse-- we have never eaten so richly! The wait staff was fascinated with us. We gave them all predictions in between courses, and some of the waiters entertained us with puppet shows and conga lines as they served the food in style. A bizarre week in our eclectic history. At almost every dinner we found ourselves sitting next to Terra Sonora. Her face glowed like an angel. As a member of the angelic realm known as "One," Terra has been channeling messages from the angels for many years and is nationally respected.

"I need to speak with you, as soon as possible," Terra whispered one evening over dessert, her voice urgent.

We converged at a private place in the lobby after dinner and sat together closely, our knees touching. With her eyes closed, Terra started channeling the realm of "One" in a thick, quite authentic Scottish brogue. Tears begin to stream down our faces.

"Greetings, dear ones! We are here to tell you that you are part of us, that you are members of The Angelic Realm of One." Terra was channeling the guides who have been helping us all of our lives. She channeled more information about our mission, describing "One" as a group of 100 beings which form an oversoul. She told us that we are two of only five members in human form here on Earth. We were amazed but shortly had to close the session, as other psychics were forming for a group photo just behind us. It was so wonderful to connect with our true angelic family.

Despite this life-altering meeting, we found ourselves continuing to struggle with debilitating fatigue and pain. The exhausting hours, little sleep and taking on clients' energy had sapped our own. We both badly needed some healing work in order to continue. As if by divine design, a woman named Gerda Lord approached us at one of the last dinners in the main dining room. She told us she had heard a great deal about us and felt a very strong connection. We also felt unusually drawn to this charming British woman, who impressed us with her kindness and wit and compassion, much like a Mary Poppins. After talking with us for quite some time, Gerda offered to do some of her healing work on us in our cabin the next day.

" I want the tremendous honor of being able to offer healing to you," Gerda told us, gripping our hands. "You are both extraordinary. The two of you have a gift that is almost beyond comprehension. You don't know how precious you are!" We felt extremely touched by her kind words. Thankfully, Gerda's healing work revived us enough to be able to be wholly present for the final day's work. Our spirit guides had no doubt brought this sensitive person to us at a time when we most needed it. On the final night of our cruise, we all gathered for a closing pow-wow in one of the seminar rooms. Andrea asked Linda to sum up the week's activities. "How about you, Linda, would you start by sharing?" she asks. Although Linda hadn't prepared anything, she stood in front of microphone. The words flowed easily, as if she were channeling them. "This has been an absolutely wonderful experience for both of us, and you all brought so much to the table. We are so very grateful to have been a part of this momentous occasion. A friend of ours out in Hollywood, Jeff, is a screenwriter. When we told him we would be on a psychic cruise, he burst out laughing and a gleeful smile lit up his face. "Oh, I get it-- it's kind of like the Love Boat, but it's "The Death Boat!"

The room exploded with laughter and there is no trace of grief on the formerly strained faces. It was hard to believe that these happy people had once been inconsolable. "He was so inspired by the idea that he is going to write a play about it!" There was thunderous applause, and after everyone had a chance to share with the group, our cruise came to a close. Happily, we both realized that through the great healing power of humor, we had been able to transform a tense and heavy mood to one of levity and hope for the future. We made many long-lasting friendships on the ship that week, and we look foward to embarking on other healing voyages on the "high seas."

Chapter Twenty-Two

GHOSTRIDER

"When the power of love overcomes the love of power, the world will know peace."

- Jimi Hendrix

Sergeant Artie Collins,* age 40, called us from Tennessee for a reading. He told us he had been praying to the Holy Mother Mary for some kind of guidance, and within five minutes of arriving home we had returned his call. "I guess my prayer was heard," said Artie, "and you and your sister are the ones who were sent to answer it." What follows is an abbreviated version of our session by phone.

Linda: Artie, have you ever flown in a combat mission?
A: Yes, I have.
L: Were you in Desert Storm? The guides are telling me you were there.
A: Yes, that is where I was last stationed.
L: Your guides are saying you lost fourteen friends in an attack when your squadron was shot down. Is this true?
A: Yes, that is exactly right. My nickname as a pilot was "Ghostrider", because the missions were flown during the night.
L: So many names are coming in. I'm getting a Butch, Carl… Tommy, Mitch, Phil, Danny… there's a George, Leroy, Freddy, Ryan, Michael, Glen and Jason…
A: That's amazing! Those were my buddies who were killed in that mission.
Terry: They say they're ordering a round of beers for you on the other side!

A: We had a round of beers the night they went up on that assignment. I never saw them again.

L: There is a message coming through from them, Artie. They are saying, "Yes, we are with you Artie, and we love you, buddy. It happened so fast, we felt no pain. Don't blame yourself because you survived."

A: Yes, I did. I felt a lot of guilt that I survived and they did not.

T: Release the guilt. Let it go. You see, guilt does not serve us, and it is a way of holding us in the past. It may be holding you back from really creating some of your dreams.

A: That is so true.

L: I'm getting a vision of a gold cross or crucifix, and it has meaning for you connected to these guys who passed.

A: Yes, the cross was given to me in the Gulf by a friend to help me process the trauma of the loss of my comrades. (Artie started to cry quietly). It was on a gold chain and I still wear it around my neck.

L: Your friends are thanking you for being so helpful. Were you helping to organize a memorial of some kind?

A: I organized the soldiers' memorial after they passed.

T: You were a soldier in the Civil War on the side of Lee, and you died as a hero in that war. You have a powerful mission to teach courage and love in this life.

A: I know that is true. I have always been fascinated by the Civil War. You have really affirmed many of my feelings today. I'm so grateful.

L: We are so honored to have been able to read for you, Artie.

*The names have been changed to protect the identities of those involved.

Chapter Twenty-Three

STRANGE UNIVERSE

Just because you're paranoid, it doesn't mean someone isn't following you.

- unknown

One day in 1994, a Los Angeles TV producer approached us about a pilot he was developing for a show called *Strange Universe* for UPN Network. Could we come down to the World Cafe, a cyber cafe in Santa Monica and participate in a group channeling the spirit of Houdini? We agreed to be a part of the filming. In attendance also were the Princess Catherine Oxenburg, and several other psychics and mediums, all huddled around a large circular table with computers connected to chat lines. We were expected to answer questions from viewers and respond online. Harry Houdini's spirit was a no-show, but we all enjoyed the evening, and met some interesting people.

One of the show's producers was a journalist named Susan Peters. We met at her request in an LA office to do an "audition" demonstrating our psychic ability for the show. She promised to do her best to create a show for us, as she was quite influential in the TV industry, and we agreed with some enthusiasm.

We proceeded to go into a reading for Susan, touching on various subjects. Peters asked us after awhile if we thought she would have children. We tuned in and told her we were sorry, but we felt she would not be physically able to conceive. The reading ended, we thanked her for her time and left. Weeks passed, and one day a friend called to say that they had seen us on an episode of *Strange Universe* the prior evening. We were quite shocked to learn that Susan Peters had secretly been taping us with hidden cameras that day! In fact, she had secretly taped many psychics from around the world, including Europe and Hawaii. On camera, it was revealed that we were the only psychics out of the many tested who correctly predicted that childbirth would be impossible for her. Apparently, Peters had a physical deformity that would prevent pregnancy, and wondered who would pick up on it.

Needless to say, we were amazed and more than a little bewildered. It was quite startling to realize that this was being done without our consent, after we had agreed to a personal reading for Peters in good faith. We had entered the world of Reality TV years before Reality TV would make its official advent. We had been "punked," but we weren't laughing. The promised show never materialized, and we never heard from Peters again. It was the first of many experiences as psychics being exploited for ratings, and not treated as human beings with feelings. We often feel that people in the industry look at us as a "dog and pony show" or circus sideshow, because they have a lack of understanding of the gifts we have, and don't know how to best utilize them.

Sadly, psychics and mediums are often misunderstood, and not respected by the media. We are hoping that as awareness grows, we will see a shift toward more sensitivity, appreciation, and humanity in handling genuine psychic talents. It would be nice to see an intelligent alternative to the glut of dating shows and survivalist shows on TV. Terry and I have the intent to create real value in people's lives, without judging or humiliating them in the process. We are ushering in an era of greater humanism, and feel that TV will eventually reflect this.

Chapter Twenty-Four

JACOB'S LADDER

"Toto, I have a feeling we're not in Kansas anymore."

- Dorothy, in The Wizard of Oz

We speak

We had just finished our lecture at an east coast Psychic Expo when a large woman in a purple mu-mu approached us. We will call her "Consuela." A remarkably rotund woman, Consuela quickly let us know that she was the queen bee of the Expo, and had been for many years. We would soon learn that Consuela is a nationally renowned healer and psychic, with an extensive education in the healing arts. We were new to the lecture circuit, and had not heard of her. "I want you to take over my clients," she announced. We were flabbergasted. "My guides have singled you out. You are the ones who are supposed to help me." She had the air of a queen bestowing the royal crown to her successors. Consuela invited us to meet her for dinner that night and bustled away, surrounded by her adoring subjects.

It was clear with one glance around her apartment that this woman was very successful. We were dying to find out what her intentions were. She showed us her press information and chattered on about her long hours doing work over the phone with an endless list of clients.

Her motivation, it seemed, was to lure people into an exorbitantly pricey workshop intensive called "The Wizard's Way" to be held at the end of the year on the remote island of Fiji. It turned out this was just one of many homes that

Consuela owned throughout the country. She wanted us to take over her lectures and clients nationally when she went on hiatus to write a book. Over dinner, we confessed that we would not be able to keep up with her business. She looked baffled. "Why not?" she asked us. Evidently, she was less psychic than people thought.

We explained about our long history of baffling, acute illnesses, and how we continued to struggle with so much chronic pain that traveling and long hours were very difficult for us, if not impossible.

She said, "What illnesses?"

Terry answered, "You name it, we had it."

"No, *you* name it," was Consuela's reply. So we did. After a half hour of listening to our lengthy health history, she invited us back to her apartment. We chatted for an hour about various things, while sprawled out on her king-sized bed. Finally, Consuela said in a somber tone, "Okay, you've been Jacob's Laddered."

"What's that?" we asked simultaneously. Now we were intrigued, yet understandably skeptical.

"It's a family curse that has been with you for generations, most likely starting with your grandmother," Consuela continued. "I very rarely see it. But I've been channelling with my guides about you all evening, and that is what my guides tell me is going on. With the Jacob's Ladder, people keep getting hit with one strange illness after another, most times with incurable illnesses, and no treatment and no doctor is able to help. Fortunately, I know how to reverse it, but it will take time." It made perfect sense to us. We had often referred to our plight as a family curse, if such a thing existed. In some cultures the word "curse" is used to describe the unknown power or pattern of energy that has control over a person.

Eckhart Tolle, in his book *The Power of Now*, describes this pattern as a "pain-body" of trapped life-energy, a negative energy field that occupies your body and your mind. It can survive only if it gets you to unconsciously identify with it. "It can then rise up, take you over, and live through you. Some pain-bodies are harmless. Others are vicious and destructive monsters, true demons. Some are physically or emotionally violent."

Trust us, you know it when you got it.

Tolle goes on to say "...the pain-body has a collective as well as a personal aspect. The personal aspect is the accumulated residue of emotional pain suffered in one's past. The collective one is the pain accumulated in the collective human psyche over thousands of years through disease, torture, war, murder, cruelty, madness, and so on. Everyone's personal pain-body (is influenced by) this collective pain-body. Anyone with a strong pain-body...may be potentially closer to enlightenment. If you are trapped in a nightmare, you will probably be more strongly motivated to awaken than someone who is just caught in the ups and downs of an ordinary dream."

According to Tolle, anything can trigger the pain, even a careless remark by someone. In Buddhism, this phenomenon is called "sansho shima," or the devilish functions within one's life and environment that come up more strongly as one develops spiritually.

This curse idea was starting to make a whole lot of sense to us. Besides, our curiosity was getting the better of us. We said goodbye to Consuela, thanking her and returned by cab to our hotel in East Manhattan. Later that week we called our friend in Miami to check on the apartment she had promised us.

"Oh, I'm so sorry, our building had a big fire and you can't stay there after all." She sounded terribly distraught. We called Consuela and she immediately offered that we could stay with her in her room during the Expo there. It all happened so fast, we weren't sure what to do. We quickly agreed.

"Call my husband at this number to get in touch with me when you arrive in Miami," Consuela offered.

We met Consuela on Friday at the hotel. It was a shabby place, built in the fifties, with the biggest lobby we had ever seen, gleaming marble floors and lots of lecture halls for speakers at the Expo. It evoked memories of a more opulent time. Booths were already set up in long rows along the hallways for vendors. There were people giving massages, psychics giving tarot card readings, while merchants sold everything from oils and gemstones to supplements and herbs. Two men in bright blue saris were "toning," making weird sounds by circling the rims of glass bowls with a wand. We found Consuela teaching a small class.

"Oh, did you find my room all right?"

"Yes, thanks, we called your husband and he told us where to go," Terry responded.

She glared viciously at us. "Stay away from my husband. I don't want any trouble."

Shocked at her unprovoked warning, we backed away, mumbling something about meeting a client, and took off. We actually never met her husband! She had told us he was a retired teacher who now helped her run her myriad workshops around the country. We felt uneasy sharing close quarters with this woman we hardly knew, and hoped she wouldn't try anything funny. We decided to stick it out, and discovered that Consuela was a workaholic who was rarely in her room. She had an insane lecture schedule and filled in every spare minute with private client sessions. This deal of taking over her business was not at all appealing to us; we did not want to be as overwhelmed with work.

During this time, we gave our own lectures, which were very well received, and returned to our room to relax. Consuela would burst into the room with a list of criticisms. We didn't have a moment's peace. Apparently, she had sent a spy to critique our lecture, a sour woman with gray hair and a bun. During our lectures Consuela would stand up and start answering questions herself, as if she were leading the lecture. This woman needed an incredible amount of attention. She threw huge parties, inviting fifty people into our tiny suite for impromptu dinner and drinks. People would gather around Consuela, who would hold court, cross-legged on the sofa, telling very funny stories for hours about what it was like to live with the aborigines. Her "henchmen" scrambled to accommodate her every wish and command, making food runs and the like. They seemed zombie-like, as though under a spell, but it was most likely due to fear. Consuela was downright scary.

At night, during the few hours Consuela did sleep, she claimed to be working on us "energetically." She had quite a reputation and we wanted to find out if her healing powers really could benefit us. We expected to feel some unusual energy or some kind of physical sensation. But the only result was Linda got a really bad headache and Terry broke out with a nasty rash. That was about it. A few weeks later, we called her to say we did not feel any better, that the pain was still there. "I've tried two dozen techniques on you. I don't know what else to do." We told her with regret that we were going to focus on developing our angelic art series, and we would not be able to take over her tour. She was extremely disappointed. Weeks later, we tried to reach her by phone, but we never heard from her again.

We do believe that The Jacob's Ladder curse exists, and that we did indeed have it, or something very much like it. We used to call it heavy karma. Were we really under a curse? We may never know. This is a common technique used by people who claim to be psychics and healers, especially those of gypsy origin. Months later, things seemed to be going a little easier for us, so who knows? We want to believe that Consuela's high magic did help us.

True or not, The Curse of Jacob's Ladder may forever remain a mystery to us. It does however serve as a symbol of our life theme: embracing our greatest obstacle and making it our greatest teacher. The physical manifestation of the collective pain-body catapulted us on our journey for truth, and has revealed to us amazing gifts we otherwise would never have known we possessed. In the process of becoming aware of the pain-body's stranglehold on us, we were able to transmute it into consciousness, and shed light on this life-long struggle. We appreciated Consuela's good intentions. Of all the healers we have worked with over the years, Consuela was undoubtedly the most interesting.

Chapter Twenty-Five

EXTREME TWINS

"Wonder Twins—Activate!"

We speak

In the last dozen years or so, we have been profiled in eleven films, mostly documentaries, which have aired in the U.S., England, and throughout Europe. Earlier this year, Unique Factuals in the UK approached us to star in the documentary "Extreme Twins," to air in England on Channel 5. Well, we are probably the most extreme twins to ever walk the planet, so we saw this as a great opportunity. It turned out to be an interesting experience for us.

The producers flew us to New York City for the filming in what had to be the coldest week of that city's winter. With the chill factor, it felt like zero degrees, and a stiff wind blew steadily across the island of Manhattan, cutting to the bone. Over the next few days, we ran around the city, filming in diners, on the busy streets of Times Square, in hotel rooms doing readings, and we were interviewed on a New York University radio show. The last dramatic day, the film crew shot us on the Staten Island ferry, with the skyline and the Statue of Liberty as a background. In the rain and fog, we were jolted by the absence of the Twin Towers, which had stood so powerfully above all other buildings. This was our first trip home since the 9/11 terrorist attacks, and the sight of the altered skyline moved us both to tears. We had at one time entertained in the World Trade Center restaurant "Windows on the World," which was the penthouse of those amazing towers, on the 103rd floor. The heroic last moments of those who died that day vividly flashed before us, as we recalled images of the colossal twin buildings going down. The fateful prediction that we had made was ignored, and clearly still haunts us. What if...?

The film "Extreme Twins" turned out to be a great success, and the producers were thrilled, or in their words, *"positively gobsmacked!"*

Shortly after we returned to Los Angeles, a producer with CBS News invited us to star in the documentary film "Psychic Children" for A&E (Arts and Entertainment Channel). They wanted to include our family in the film, as testimony to what living with psychic children had been like for them. The film aired a dozen times on four networks and was very successful. More importantly, this was the first time our prediction of the World Trade Center terrorist attacks had been aired since that interview with Art Bell in 1999 – five years after 9/11 actually occurred. The response was tremendous.

Psychic children fall into several categories, and several extensive studies have been done defining the different types: Indigo children, Rainbow children, and Crystal children. Since the 1970's, more and more psychic children have been recognized and all of them seem to share certain qualities and "special" abilities of perception, intuition, personality traits and gifts of seeing. Many are misdiagnosed with ADD or autism, because adults have not yet learned how to respond to the needs of these sensitive children, who are here on Earth to dissolve the old paradigms and ways of being.

Linda was awakened in the early morning hours the night before the filming. She glanced at the clock and it said three a.m. After some time of tossing and turning, she had a nagging urge to get out of bed and channel a message from the Psychic Children. Linda remembered that she had just that week bought a beautiful little book handmade in Nepal. It was made of hand-pressed parchment paper and bound with a little brown string and wooden bead, and Linda thought it had a charming, antiquated feeling about it. Linda began to channel and the writing flowed. Before she knew it, Linda found that she had written a seven-page message from The Psychic Children of the fourth dimension. What follows is a brief excerpt.

"Yes, hello, dear one," it began. "We are coming to you at this early morning hour to thank you for being a speakerphone on behalf of all the Psychic Children of the world. We are most grateful for your gift of channeling our collective voice for all to hear and understand. Yes, we come to the dense energy of the Earth plane from the highly tuned vibration of the fourth dimension as high teachers for the suffering beings who dwell here. As psychic twins, you and Terry have a high resonance together which enables you both to receive information from the fourth and fifth dimensional planes. You have a mission of accelerating consciousness on Earth and balancing the energy of the planet for millions of people in a time of deep chaos and suffering... The Psychic Children are helping to birth a new destiny for your planet, a new evolution of consciousness if you will. You are one pair in a matrix of light beings who have chosen to come to Earth as part of a profound spiritual transformation heretofore unknown in this density. You are helping the planet to awaken from a dream of the illusion of separation.

"The Psychic Children hold a key to this awakening which is at its heart a message of truth and pure divine love... Their pure hearts are helping to balance the energies on the third-dimensional plane and resore sanity in the new millennium. You are helping to break deeply negative mind patterns that have existed for eons. Fear not! We are surrounding you both in great love and embracing you in one giant Cosmic hug! More trust is required now than ever before! Be so confident. The year of greatest impact will be 2012, a most powerful zenith. You are assisting the gifted children to step into their power and begin speaking on behalf of the lost… We are most proud of our twins as you forge a path for your planet toward a new consciousness, toward wholeness, integration and enlightenment. Self love is the goal for your human friends who feel that material possessions are the answer to their inner void… Accept them with unconditional love if possible. They are blind to what is true and real. Ego has a way of creating mass illusion on your plane. So many stuck in a place of wanting and striving and attachment… Wayshowers, be so happy to be among the ones to usher in a new era of blessings and divine love. We are with you as your journey unfolds. Many blessings, The Realm of One (on behalf of The Psychic Children).”

TRADING SPACES

On our birthday, January 12th, Terry woke up with the thought, “Gee, I wish we could redecorate this apartment.” Twenty minutes later, at about 8:00 a.m., the phone rang. The Learning Channel was calling to ask us to star on a psychic special for *Trading Spaces*! This has for years been one of cable TV’s biggest hit shows and of course, we were tickled pink to be invited to participate. The premise is that one couple trades homes with another couple (called a “team”) and in just four days, redecorates one of their rooms for under two thousand dollars. It’s a home-improvement show with a twist—will the couple like their new room or hate it? Some people do hate the result, and never speak to their friends again. Fun for the whole family!

We had to find another psychic who would want to trade with us, and we found her—our friend Melissa. She and her husband Guillermo rent an apartment in Beverly Hills, and courageously agreed to join us. Melissa is a gifted intuitive and also an interior decorator who had been wanting to start her own business. After many weeks of preparation, TLC arrived with their huge *Trading Spaces* truck for the taping. This is basically a two-ton Home Depot store on eighteen wheels, which they drove clear across the country--just for us!

We had the amazing opportunity to work together with the star decorators of the show--Doug Wilson and Frank Bielec, as well as celebrity carpenters Carter Oosterhouse and Faber Dewar. Doug is handsome, with a caustic wit. He is known as the taskmaster of all the designers on the show, and we worked closely with him on Melissa's décor. Frank is like a jolly Santa, warm and eccentric, extremely talented. He worked with the other team and in just four days, they transformed our rather boring apartment into a custom showcase fit for, well--psychic twins! We couldn't have been more delighted with the result. Our living room and dining room had been redone in soft hues of lavender, with brand new eggplant colored sofas and dark wood furniture, complete with a crystal chandelier and diaphanous, flowing drapes! Meanwhile, we transformed Melissa's home as well, even creating original artwork for her walls.

On day two of the makeover, Doug was admiring Linda's automatic writing, and suddenly said, "Can you do this on a large scale, say… six feet tall?" Linda assured him that she could. She told him that for a long time she had dreamed of producing her automatic writing as a large-scale artwork. Clearly, we were working in synchronicity with Doug, and he seemed genuinely inspired. Since we were under a tight schedule, we had to act quickly. Doug drove us both to the nearest art store and we got the necessary materials for the project. When we got back to the apartment, Linda went to work as the film crew documented her process. She wrote a channeled poem from Melissa's spirit guides, and painstakingly transferred it to the large board, with Terry assisting. The final piece was covered with a thick sheet of plexiglass that had been cut to fit, and was mounted on the wall in Melissa's "psychic parlor." Doug said on camera that this was the room he felt proudest of, in all his six years of doing the show.

The taping itself was vaudeville at its best. We used to dream of having a sitcom, but reality TV can provide the perfect forum for improv comedy, and we were right at home in this venue. We cracked jokes with the hosts and crew, painted walls and bookshelves, created window treatments, gave improvisational readings to twenty people, whipped up artwork… Linda even learned how to wield a circular saw! This was truly a three-ring circus—what great fun. Never give up on your dream, because it will likely manifest in a way that you could not possibly plan or expect.

Psychic Detectives

We speak

Last September, producers of the CBS show *The Insider* brought us in as psychic detectives on a high-profile missing persons case. The longtime boyfriend of famous singer Olivia Newton-John had mysteriously vanished June 30, 2005 without a trace. Patrick Kim McDermott, a handsome man with model-good-looks, was last seen in San Pedro, California, on a private fishing boat called *"Freedom."* We usually follow with interest the development of missing persons cases and unsolved murders, and this one had caught our attention. We both felt strongly that we could be of help in cracking the case, and agreed to taping the CBS segment the next day.

Early the next morning, a shiny black limo picked us up and drove us to a fishing dock in San Pedro, the location where Patrick went missing. It was a lovely,warm morning and the sun glanced sharply off the sun-bleached fishing boats. The CBS camera crew set up and interviewed us for over an hour, with *The Freedom* as a backdrop. News reports said that his family and authorities suspected that he had either been murdered and thrown overboard, or that he had committed suicide, or accidentally drowned.

The perky blonde host, Lara Spencer, opened the segment. "The Psychic Twins may be able to solve what the cops can't."

Linda spoke first. "There's no dead body here."

"We don't sense death energy here," Terry concurred.

"We feel that he faked his own disappearance. It was pre-meditated. He's not in this country right now. He's gone south and he's in Mexico," said Linda.

"There will be a reunion with Olivia Newton-John, and we feel positive about that," added Terry, "but there are a lot of painful issues there."

We knew we were taking a huge risk going on a national show in what was at the time the number one mystery in TV news, due to Newton-John's world-wide celebrity. After all, a case like this is extremely unusual. But we call it as we see it.

That episode of CBS' *The Insider* aired nationally, four times that weekend. We had half expected to hear from Olivia or from Patrick's family, but there was no communication from them at all. This man had left behind a young son, and our hearts went out to him. A few weeks later we did receive an email—from the owners of *The Freedom*, the fishing boat where Patrick was last seen. *The Freedom* owners thanked us profusely for getting them off the hook. For months, the police had, in their words, "made their lives a living hell," suspecting that they had some involvement in Patrick's disappearance. It was very rewarding to hear that we had put their hearts and minds at ease—but the case didn't end there.

Nine months after we went public with our impressions, we were relaxing at home watching Fox News Channel. To our astonishment, the news anchor of *The Lineup* reported that four credible witnesses had independently spotted Patrick McDermott—*in Mexico!* He had been seen on the remote Baja Peninsula in the resort town of Cabo San Lucas. A bar owner, a surf camp owner and a businessman had reported the sightings to police. The bar owner said McDermott told him he was working on a private fishing boat. A sun visor was found on the scene containing forensic evidence that could incriminate McDermott. A grand jury is currently underway that will investigate his disappearance. When apprehended, Mr. McDermott could be charged with fraud, plotting his own disappearance and non-payment of thirty-thousand dollars in back child support. Olivia Newton-John is expected to have to answer some tough questions if brought in front of a grand jury.

In a recent appearance on Australian TV, Olivia Newton-John commented on the sightings of Patrick. This quote is from *The Australian*:

*Olivia Newton-John has broken her silence over reports her missing boyfriend was in hiding in Mexico, saying she would be thrilled if it were true. Patrick McDermott, who was with Newton-John for nine years, was thought to have drowned off the coast of California almost a year ago until **recent evidence suggested he may have faked his death and is in hiding in Mexico.***

"It's obviously very distressing for everyone in the family. We just miss him and love him and we'd be thrilled if it's true," Newton-John told Australian television today.

This may be the first time that psychics have correctly predicted on TV the location of a missing person where it was later verified. In February 2003 we had correctly predicted in a national magazine that Scott Peterson would be found guilty of murdering his wife Laci Peterson (at the time, he had not yet been considered a suspect), and that Laci would be found in a body of water. Several months later, her body and that of her unborn son washed ashore.

The Court TV program *Psychic Detectives* profiles true cases where psychics have been enlisted to help investigators solve mysteries. Often when a case goes cold, a psychic is contacted by the family to help the police go in a direction that may have been overlooked.

Psychic detectives can provide a new light on a case, whether it involves a murder, kidnapping or a missing person. In much the same way as a criminal profiler provides a new way to assess a killer and his motives, the psychic can provide insightful details for the police.

We have to admit, there is something that is very rewarding about doing psychic detective work. The truth is, very few police departments utilize the help of psychic investigators, even on cold cases. The use of intuitives in criminology is still highly controversial. Often, psychics are brought in to assist police only as a last resort, and many are not acknowledged for their help by investigators. Often we will call the police tip lines with our impressions, but they usually ignore us. We find it somewhat laughable when we see the FBI, police, and private detectives sending dive teams in, when we can see clearly that the body is buried in the mountains! We feel that the use of intuitives can be an important investigative tool for private detectives. If only the police would involve reputable psychics more often, a lot more crimes would be solved, and a lot more quickly.

Chapter Twenty-Six

SLAYING THE DRAGONS

"It is our light, not our darkness, that most frightens us."

- Marianne Williamson

Linda speaks

None of us can really know the depth of our karma, what kinds of causes we have each made in past incarnations. Our lives are eternal, and this life is like an eye blink in the overall scheme. We are assured of changing our destinies if we choose to do the spiritual work. I have realized through so many hardships that everything depends on our attitude. I once read about a man who was totally paralyzed except for his eyes. This remarkable man wrote a book, and had even more goals he wanted to attain, though all he could do was *blink!* We felt the same way about persevering and pursuing our dreams in spite of our illness.

Years ago, I worked in a large retail store. Along with numerous other young employees, I was demeaned and harassed by managers with drug and alcohol problems, who had no compassion whatsoever. The managers seemed to delight in blatantly putting people down. When I could take the abuse no longer, I was forced to quit. A friend encouraged me to file a lawsuit for damages and lost wages. I did file a suit, a process that lasted almost two years. I had confidence that I would be victorious if I stayed strong in my faith. I felt as though I had a steel will during the grueling ten-hour depositions, during which the lawyer for the defense tried to demonize me and used a technique of character assassination to make me appear unstable and unreliable. Even while the accused lied almost constantly under questioning, I never stopped sending light to them.

I won, and received a small settlement. It was a powerful experience in standing up for myself, speaking the truth, and taking back my power. I was also able to forgive all the people involved in the situation, and take responsibility for what happened so that I could release the feeling of being a victim. I know that I would not have won had my attitude been one of resentment and anger, seeking punishment. It was only in the challenging of my fear and negativity that I was able to demonstrate the result I did.

Since that time, both Terry and I have been challenged in extreme ways by people who either feared or misunderstood our intentions with the psychic and healing work. We have been called on to slay some pretty ugly dragons, especially in the TV industry where talent is used, wadded up and tossed aside.

Many people are so rigidly attached to beliefs from the past that they close their minds to anything truly new. According to scientist Gary Schwartz, the scholars of Copernicus' time refused to even look through the newly developed telescopes to see what the instruments were revealing. Skepticism is a strange beast.

Even in the Buddhist organization, many of our leaders in faith tried to stop us or discourage us from practicing our intuitive work. One leader said, "You shouldn't call yourselves "The Psychic Twins." Why not call ourselves what we are? Another leader came over and threw our crystals in the trash can (we promptly retrieved them). Many old-school Buddhists fear psychic work as much as some Christians do, simply due to a lack of understanding. There is a lot of superstition and attachment to dogma. It was with great sadness that we chose eventually to leave the organization that we had helped to pioneer, because we felt so judged and controlled. This is the opposite of the philosophy of Buddhism, which embraces all people. In the last five or six years, the organization has made a greater effort to embrace gays and those of us who are not "the norm," in an attempt to expand. Hopefully, this trend will continue.

Recently, we were featured speakers at a health expo in Portland, Oregon. A standing-room-only crowd packed the lecture hall to hear us speak about how people can develop their own psychic abilities. We also did some demonstrations of our gift for audience members who had questions. The lecture went very well, and afterward, many approached us to find out how to receive a private session. Shortly after we had left, we were shocked to hear that several people were spreading rumors about our "psychically attacking them" while we were in Portland. It took on the feeling of a witch hunt. Someone even accused us of having used our psychic energy to cause an elderly woman to fall and hurt her hip. We had never even met her!

Perhaps the most surprising thing was that several of our biggest persecutors were healing practitioners in the community, who practiced metaphysical principals. We felt like we were in some kind of bizarre movie (remember *Carrie*, or the movie *Powder?*) When we confronted the perpetrators about it, they became defensive and angry. It is a sad reality that ignorance breeds fear. Even now, we still encounter intelligent people who mistrust and resent psychic abilities in others. This may explain why very few psychics come out publicly. It takes courage to challenge these deep-rooted judgments and fears.

Chapter Twenty-Seven

TRUSTING IT

"After all, what is reality anyway? Nothing but a collective hunch."
- Lily Tomlin, The Search for Signs of Intelligent Life

We speak

We had heard from two of our friends about a healer named Jean-Michel, a French man who travels to many countries. His work involves purifying energetic fields in a variety of dimensions, elevating one's vibration which facilitates the state of the soul's balance. When the opportunity came up to see him in Santa Monica, California, we called immediately to schedule an appointment. Jean-Michel works in tandem with him partner Miriane, who takes notes during the session. Driving to the appointment, a steady drizzle fell against gray skies, and Terry was almost overcome with physical pain and fatigue. Intuitively, we knew this was going to be a most profound event for both of us.

Terry went first, sitting opposite Jean-Michel in a straight, hard-backed chair while Linda waited upstairs. He was a diminutive man in his late fifties with a soft, priest-like persona. He held a Y-shaped "antenna device" which looked like a dowsing rod, with which he measures one's energetic field and spiritual levels. Quietly saying prayers in French, his hands trembling noticibly, he began to work on Terry with energetic healing. She felt anxious as she struggled to make sense of Jean-Michel's broken English. After about thirty minutes, Jean-

Michel worked with a deck of tarot cards and addressed some of Terry's concerns.

Linda went into the room as Terry exited. When asked to describe her illness, she went into some detail (as Terry had) about her lifelong struggle with chronic illnesses that seemed to baffle doctors and healers alike. Bowing his head, Jean-Michel began reciting prayers in French, and moved his hands as he did so. After a short time, he stood behind Linda and worked around her head, continuing to pray. Miriane joined him, doing reiki (energy) healing in front of Linda. When they finished the healing, Jean-Michel spoke softly to Miriane, who translated the assessment for Linda. With surprise, Miriane exclaimed that Linda had experienced a most unusual expansion during the session. They told her that her energy could now balance that of nine million peoples' suffering on the planet. They explained that our illnesses were connected to past lives, and that Linda was releasing deep pain for her soul's evolution. Jean-Michel told her that he recognized the energy of Archangel Michael around her, and said that he also works with this ascended master's energy. Linda was informed that she was in an expansion process that involved "moving out of the field of fear to become the light." "Love your body and love your pain," he told her. "You will be experiencing some discomfort over the next three months as all of your subtle bodies (etheric, emotional, mental-causal and spiritual bodies) go through a purification process."

Linda then asked them how she could be of help to them with her own abilities. Did they have a problem she could help with? They did, and she gave them an impromptu reading concerning several urgent matters the two were confronting. "You are a very good psychic," said Miriane with a warm smile, encouraged. "You have expressed several things other psychics have told us as well."

Two days later, we were taking our daily walk in the beautiful hills of our neighborhood. Terry said a silent prayer to the angels and nature devas (spirits of nature) for an omen, a sign that we were on the right track. Within minutes a bright Monarch butterfly circled us, followed by several more. Then, to our utter amazement, scores of butterflies swarmed out from behind the homes and trees on the hills, descending upon us by the hundreds, then thousands! They came out of nowhere, in our direction. A magnificent and colorful swirl of winged creatures surrounded us. We were mesmerized, enchanted, and completely amazed by this magical phenomenon. Their numbers increased as we walked another hour towards home. This was undeniably a powerful oracle from our angelic guides, the realm of "One" letting us know that a great transformation had occurred for us. The butterfly phenomena continued for two days, and just as quickly vanished. It was truly a sign of blessings to come.

* * *

Oprah Winfrey calls the intuition "our wise self." Oprah once said about herself, "I was born to greatness." We always had the sense, even as children, that we were born to make a big difference in this world, not for few but for many. We feel very fortunate to have been able to do this. We now have clients in all 50 states, twenty European countries, and Australia and Japan as well. But hoping would not have been enough to accomplish our dreams and goals. It took decades of steady effort, practice, and spiritual work to trust ourselves and to develop our gifts and abilities.   For many years, we met with a lot of opposition. Our field is the only one that has been labeled "the work of the devil," with the exception of perhaps the legal field. This fearful attitude is due to faulty teachings and misconceptions about what psychic work and mediumship is. It is mainly due to ignorance, a lack of understanding. We knew that we were meant to be a bridge of understanding, and our mission has been to educate people about the value of intuition and emotions and make psychic work more accessible to all. Everyone has intuition, and some have true psychic gifts, or gifts of channeling or communicating with the spirit world. The problem arises when one judges, fears, or blocks the messages he or she is receiving from the spirit realm. The day before 9/11 occurred, we were taping a pilot for FOX TV called *State of Mind.* Terry said on camera, "Trusting your intuition could mean the difference between life and death." The very next day, on 9/11, hundreds of people survived because they listened to their intuition, skipping work or going in late. Some chose to stay home because they had a "gut feeling." In this case, their intuition saved their lives. We can't see electricity, but we believe in it. We can't understand the function of breathing, but we believe in it. We cannot see the spirit world, but it is there. Spirits surround us invisibly. Even atheists have spirit guides! The more we acknowledge their presence, the more psychically sensitive we can become. In his book *Psychic Living*, Andrei Ridgeway says that the reason many people have difficulty achieving their dreams is "that we have been conditioned to express only a very small part of our character. At some point in our lives we were so brutally defined by those around us that we cut off vital parts of ourselves in exchange for love and acceptance." Society's obsession with logic and reason have in effect crippled the human intuitive spirit. As a consequence, our society undervalues esoteric and mystical faculties. People nowadays spend more time and energy on tooth whitening and plastic surgery when their energy would be better spent on spiritual investigation, learning how to know and love themselves from the inside out. More than ever, each of us must learn to reconnect with our inner voice. Because we had no teachers in this work, we had to learn to trust our "spirit teachers." We are spirit-taught, meaning that all of our techniques including the automatic writing that we do came to us from our angels and our spirit guides. We laugh when people ask, "How accurate are you?" or "What is your percentage of accuracy?" We are two of the few psychics in the world who have a proven track record, and we have predicted almost every major event that has already occurred in this new millennium, either on TV, radio or published in national magazines. Our record speaks for itself. The misconception is that because a person is psychic, he or she must know "everything." We do not pretend to be the "Voice of God." Prophets act as harbingers of change, so that people might protect themselves, and take measures to circumvent a tragedy. The purpose is not to "be right" but to help people. "All truth," said Arthur Schopenhauer, "passes through three stages. First, it is ridiculed. Second, it is violently opposed. Third, it is accepted as being self-evident."

How did we know 9/11 was going to happen, while the entire so-called "intelligence agency" of the U.S. government (the CIA and FBI) missed it? Why did no one listen? We will never really know.

But we promise you this, they are listening to us now.

Chapter Twenty-Eight

INTEGRATION

American Aborigine

with no antelope in sight
I will be fed
with no clear path
I will divine the way
living by my wits
sacrificing my soul for a dream
I will learn somehow
to explain the unexplainable
to know the unknowable
to teach the unteachable
encourage the unencouragable.
I will plant seeds of life in tragic soil
I will birth a new destiny.

- Linda Jamison

We speak

Carl Jung said that modern man, in the process of becoming civilized, lost his ability to be intuitive, to perceive the sacred, magical aspects of life. We know that in our work as artists, performers and psychics, we are helping people to awaken to their own mystical side. The ancient cultures had connection with the intuitive realm, gaining access to the higher realms through vision quests, dreams and shamanism. In this crucial time of world suffering, we are each being asked to go deeper inside our hearts and to birth something powerful. We may do this through raising conscious children, or creating awareness of ecology, or contributing in some way to the evolution of a new consciousness.

Gary Zukav, in *Seat of the Soul*, talks about the great minds of thinkers like Albert Einstein, Carl Jung, and William James. He said that what motivated these men (whom he refers to as mystics) was in fact a great vision beyond what the personality could imagine. "Each of us in now being drawn, in one way or another, to that same great vision... more than a vision, it is an emerging force, as an authentic power that moves the force fields of this Earth of ours."

The work we do as psychics has been unacceptable in mainstream society for 3000 years. The language and information of the goddesses and priests, once ritualized by religions and mystery schools, and made esoteric by a controlling patriarchal church, can now become available to all beings. Quantum physics, neurology and molecular biology are beginning to validate what psychics and mystics have been teaching for centuries. What we want to create is a new vanguard of thought and creativity that can open up people to a new level of being and communicating in our time.

As part of a counterculture that for too long has suffered persecution from a fearful patriarchal society, the artists, healers and intuitives are now starting to gain widespread acceptance and validation. Our visions challenge existing paradigms, and break down limiting belief systems. We are collectively ushering in the Aquarian Age, a new phase of evolution expressing concepts of balance, compassion, teamwork and partnership. As earth energies are quickening toward the year 2012, the last year of the Mayan calendar, we are playing an important role in building a bridge of understanding for generations to follow.

We have been told that in our working together as identical twins, we possess a phenomenal intuitive empathy, a mysterious synergy that is exponentially much greater than we are as individuals. "High Strangeness" is a term used in paranormal and UFO research for years. It is a term for a phenomenon that defies conventional physics, something so peculiar that nothing can make sense of it. We feel that we embody this concept. It is risky and difficult to go against the social "norm"--one risks rejection, judgment, anger, abandonment and persecution. We can testify that we have experienced all of these effects as long as we've been practicing metaphysics.

Christ said, "In my Father's house are many mansions" or dimensions. We feel this refers to the planes of our multi-dimensional universe. From the dense physical planes of the material universe to the seventh level or Cosmic Plane, where the soul finally merges with Source energy, or God, we all progress in myriad roles divinely designed to heal the splintered parts of our selves. That is to say, the soul selects in each life a unique set of personality traits and potential conditions for the purpose of experiencing and evolving, with the ultlmate goal of achieving mastery. We hope that in communing with the Akasha and Angelic Realms, we can be a light on the path, and perhaps inspire a deeper look into the cosmic matrix of our lives.

The champion wheelchair racer Jim Knaub once said, " Pain will take you on a journey, and in that journey can be hope. Why walk when you can fly?" Today as we write this, our health is improving. We must be diligent about our nutrition, exercise, and emotional therapy, trying never to indulge in depression and frustration. We are an ongoing work in progress (we say we're still "under construction") and we appreciate every small step forward, celebrating even the little victories.

We came to realize that our disabilities were only as limiting as we chose. As a result of challenging our physical limitations, we developed our internal, spiritual abilities-- the power of mind over matter-- and this became our greatest gift, our authentic power.

We were separated at Earth, and through adversity we found integration with ourselves, each other, and the universe.

Chapter Twenty Nine

DANCING WITH POSSIBILITY

"We must pursue knowledge, without any interference of our addictions or judgments, and then we will manifest knowledge of realities… and experience it in new ways, new chemistries, new holograms and new elsewheres of thought beyond our wildest dreams."

- J.Z. Knight

The question we get most often is *"but how do you DO that?"* Listen, folks, even quantum physics has no clear answers to the big questions, and this is a big question! In this chapter, we will explain how we developed our extraordinary psychic abilities, and the methods we use to "attune" to subtle frequencies. We will explain some of the reasons that you may be resisting the process of really tuning into your own inner voice, and share with you simple methods that can help you develop your own intuitive potential. First, we invite you to answer this question: do you want better relationships, greater abundance, better health, a job you love, and a sense of inner peace? If you have all of these things, you may not need to read this chapter, but most people are desiring expansion, growth, and knowledge in at least one aspect of their lives. The information we are about to share with you in this book will help you to do all of these things and more.

As stated earlier in the book, we grew up in the sixties, in a small country town outside of Philadephia called West Chester. Our parents were watercolor masters with a growing reputation, so our childhood was imbued with an appreciation for painting, art, and antiques. In fact, every member of our small and eccentric family are artists, writers, or painters. But there were no psychics in our town and certainly no teachers of life's mysteries. We had never even heard of psychics until we were adults. Even though we were born with many artistic talents and intuitive gifts, no one in our environment was equipped to help us develop them. We have devoted our lives to a spiritual quest to understand our special path as intuitives and teachers, but we ourselves had no formal training in psychic work. Our gifts were developed through our constant intention to connect with spirit energies.

You may not want to be psychic twins or world prophets, but you can develop your own gifts of intuition to find your true path, do the work you love, and manifest your dreams. Won't you join us as we teach you how to dance with possibility?

We start every day with meditation. Years ago we did a TV show with a famous medium, and we asked him if he did any kind of meditation before reading people. His response was "No, never." A year later he came out with a book on meditation! Suddenly, he was an expert. We have practiced various forms of meditation for twenty-five years, and it is the most important foundation of psychic work. We have chanted a mantra every day. That mantra is, in our opinion, the Mercedes of all mantras: Nam Myoho Renge Kyo. The unexpected result was a greatly enhanced sensitivity to others; we found we were making wiser decisions, and all of our psychic gifts gradually expanded. Buddhism teaches that the most important benefits of the practice are not "conspicuous," but "inconspicuous benefits." This simply means benefits or qualities that you can't see or touch such as well-being, joy, health, compassion and the like. In this very material culture, that is a tough sell. Many people think that the goal is the house, the sportscar, a fat salary---material trappings-- but these were not our goals. We were always most interested in human potential, bettering ourselves, and being of service to others. A happy life will center on your ability to master these as well.

There is no "right way" to meditate, no secret formula. Through exploration you can find a method that works best for you. Meditation is the best way to be in "receiving mode." To become powerful manifestors in our lives, we must be willing to open up to receive spirit guidance and positive energy. The goal of meditation is to quiet your mind to hear your inner voice and the voice of spirit. As thoughts come to mind, gently release them like leaves floating downstream, focusing on the breath. Our friends have marveled at what slow eaters we are. The two of us are usually the last to finish a meal, while others gulp their food without even tasting it. That is because we have reached a point that everything we do is a meditation. We try to bring a mindfulness to everything we do.

Many people tell us that they can't meditate because their minds are "too busy." This is simply resistance, because you are in the habit of resisting well-being. You have even more reason to meditate, because it will help you to quiet your mind and let go of cerebral activity. If sitting quietly for a length of time is too difficult for you, yoga or a walking meditation may be the best way to start. Take a long walk in nature, noticing and appreciating the flowers, birds, and beauty around you. Many of us have lost the "art" of observation. We started practicing Hatha and Kundalini yoga in our early twenties, and we recommend it highly. People who live at a slower, more calm pace tend to be more open to psychic guidance, and are generally more effective in their daily lives than those who rush around unconsciously, not noticing the sounds, signals and smells around them.

As we go through our day, we do many things to stay centered and grounded in the present moment. We eat healthy food to keep our energy level up. A diet full of colorful vegetables and fruits, whole grains and protein is the best way to detoxify your body and raise your vibration. We rarely drink alcohol, and have never smoked cigarettes or anything else. Alcohol and drugs will create a veil between you and spirit, blocking your ability to receive—this is important to recognize. We find it strange that many people who practice healing and psychic work are chain-smokers, heavy drinkers or overeaters. These habits are self-defeating, and will definitely create a roadblock to manifesting the things you want to achieve or attract to you. Remember, the body is a temple, the conduit or instrument through which spirit resonates. Your body communicates to you whether or not you are aligned with your ideal or right life, so it is important to detox and start to communicate with your body. Many of us are the "walking wounded," disconnected from our physical bodies because we have repressed our emotions and feelings for years. In order to develop your intuition and magnetize your dreams, it is necessary to heal your past emotional wounds and listen to your feelings.

All day long, we tend to laugh a lot. Our humor not only saved our lives, it raises our life condition and speeds up our vibration so that we can attract things we want and need. If worry or negative emotions come up, we try to notice these feelings and shift our focus to what we want to feel or create. You see, pure positive energy is always flowing through us as long as we don't resist it. Worry and angry thoughts, even self-doubt, will slow down your vibration and block your spiriitual progress.

Before we do a reading, we say prayers and do visualizations, calling in our angels and guides. This enables us to reconnect to Source energy, or "co-create" with spirit. A key part of the attunement process is the ability that we have to "detach" from our conscious mind, to step aside and let spirit inform us. This way we know that our own thoughts will not influence the answers or predictions. Then we imagine white, blue, violet and silver light surrounding us like a cocoon of protective energy. We ask to connect with the guides of the person we are reading, and we are ready to begin preparing the reading.

Whether we work by phone or in person, we take several minutes to "tune in" to the energy field of the person who we will be reading. The impressions we receive may be either a visual image or symbol (clairvoyance), a thought or idea (claircognizance), a feeling (clairsentience), or all of the above simultaneously. We work multi-dimensionally and we believe that our readings and our voices have healing power, as countless clients have told us. Therefore, it is not simply the words we speak that are important, but the healing that occurs on many subtle dimensions. People have often commented to us that they feel an unusual sense of calm and inner peace after a session with us.

Gary Zukav writes about how we are moving from five-sensory beings (using only five senses) to multi-sensory beings, and we can all transform how we affect our reality, our environment, and other people by paying attention to our emotions and thoughts. For some reason people in our culture have been taught to suppress or deny their emotions, as though they are bad, scary monsters like boogey men in a dark room! But in a supportive environment, feeling and revealing our emotions becomes less frightening, even cathartic. All that emotional baggage really blocks one's intuition from flowing, and it is time to let it go—now! If you are fearful, sad, guilty or angry about something, acknowledge it. Feel the feelings around the emotion. This will help you break through to a new level of being and experiencing.

If you are uncomfortable verbalizing your feelings, writing is a very effective way of getting in touch them. We advise our clients to write their feelings out in a journal. Buy a beautiful book and keep it beside your bed. In the morning or before bedtime, write how you are feeling, what is bothering you. Don't edit or reread it. It is also a good idea to have a separate book or journal in which to write down all the things you are grateful for. This is sometimes called a "Blessings Journal." Our thoughts expand, so if you focus on the good things you want more of, you will attract them-- it is a spiritual law.

Everyone is too busy these days, overscheduled, with carpools and kids and too many obligations on top of working full time. This habit of overworking is perhaps the biggest block to developing one's intuition, and it makes connecting to spirit nearly impossible. The truth is that people tend to overwork or stay overly busy to avoid feeling. We encourage everyone to slow down, simplify your life, learn to say no to others. Set boundaries. Let go of your need to be the perfect mom, the perfect boss, the perfect anything. When you clearly have this intention, and make time to nurture yourself, you will be surprised at how happy your spirit helpers will be (not to mention everyone around you whom you have been stressing out). Your family and friends will notice the shift in you immediately.

We find that men in particular are more addicted to work, to proving themselves, and society has taught men that it is not masculine to feel. It is time to relearn faulty teachings. When men are able to slow down and pay more attention to their feelings they find they are able to contribute more at home and in the workplace. Once you are able to slow down and tune into your feelings, you open your consciousness to hear your inner wisdom and the whispers of angels. In this expanded state, you can bring through higher energies for inspiration, instruction or comfort. You will begin to think in new ways.

We rarely do a reading without addressing the issue of creativity. During a session with us, we don't ask you what your talents and interests are-- your spirit guides tell us what they are! Having a passion (or more than one) is one of the most crucial steps to psychic development we know. Because we have been artists, painters, singers, performers and writers all our lives, we are especially tuned into the artistic gifts of others. But the problem we find most of our clients have is that they either have gifts that they don't use, or they have blocked their passion completely. If we ask, "what is your passion?" many will look at us blankly or cannot think of a single hobby or creative activity they like to do.

The solution? Have more fun! Take classes in things you have never done or never imagined doing. Set a goal to try a new creative activity like gardening, writing, or dancing for thirty days. Through doing this exercise, you will be surprised at how your attitude can shift in all areas of your life. You will find that you are more present for others, more relaxed and more self-expressed. People may even tell you you look younger! Creativity helps you to access the child within, enabling you to approach life's problems and challenges more joyfully, gracefully, with a renewed sense of confidence. Your walls come down, and you will become more open, more free. You will become more intuitive.

Melanie came to us with a problem many people share. She felt she was at a crossroads in her life as she was turning sixty. She was getting her masters in art education after many years of dreaming about doing it. Having survived two abusive marriages and raised three boys, she wondered how she could create a life she really loved. She had taught for twenty years, and wanted to get a job as an art teacher yet she felt stuck in an old conversation about what she could create.

In speaking with her, it became clear that she had some limiting conversations going on about what a woman her age could get in the way of a job. She said that most colleges were interested only in hiring young people with less experience, so they could pay less. We coached her in shifting her belief about what was possible. We taught her how to meditate daily, and to flow her energy toward the feeling place of having a job she loved. The Universe wants to support your success as you commit to new conversations about what is possible, we told her. The old "tapes" about what might happen, what she feared could happen, were siimply not serving her anymore. We urged her to know and trust that she deserves to be hired for the best teaching position doing what she loves, with a kind, supportive boss and coworkers, and students who appreciate her.

Melanie seemed to perk up as soon as she heard this new directive. It resonated with her on a deep soul level. We mentioned how she was sabotaging her best intentions by languaging negatively about what could happen for her. The shift would require deeper levels of trust and commitment, we told her. Let go of the reasons and excuses for not being, doing and having what you want. Let go of the old identity you cling to that says your dream is out of reach. Affirm to yourself that you will be honored, respected, rewarded, supported for your work in the world. Your brain and body neurology actually will shift accordiing to the thoughts you flow. Your llife will begin to work. Things will begin to fall in place very synchronistically, very naturally as you open to receive the abundance that is your birthright.

Opportunities will flow in to you as you stretch the boundaries of your consciousness and ability to receive. Linda told Melanie that she had a sense of her oldest son being "lost" somehow. Melanie confided that she had chills when Linda said that. She had given up her baby son for adoption when she was 21, and had recently found him after many years of searching. He had indeed been lost to her, she said tearfully.

Terry said she had a feeling her ex-husband had passed of lung cancer. Yes, Melanie confirmed this. "Was he an alcoholic?" Terry asked. "Yes, he was." Terry encouraged Melanie that it was time to take back the power that she had given away to her husband six years ago. "That is exactly when it happened," Melanie said. "I'm ready now." Suddenly, Terry had a psychic impression of Melanie traveling around the country, doing paintings for people of their angels and spirit guides. It was a more creative solution for Melanie to be an artist and to also get to do what she wanted most—travel. When we ended the conversation, Melanie's energy and attitude had dramatically shifted into one of joy, hope and optimism. She realized that she could lead a truly creative life of her own choosing, while getting to do all the things she dreamed of.

Laura was stuck in a bad marriage with a husband who was cheating on her. We got to the root of the problem right away. We had the sense that she was afraid to leave him, because she was terrified of being alone. She confirmed that yes, she had never been on her own, and had a teenage pregnancy. We explained to her that she felt it was her job to "fix" her husband, and that she needed to start by forgiving him for the affair. Women are caretakers by nature, and we often feel it is our job to fix the people and relationships around us, to keep the peace and make everyone happy. This is simply not possible! It is never our job to fix others. We can be a spiritual and healing influence on others, but first and foremost we need to take care of ourselves. This is not self-centered or selfish, it is having what we call a "centered self."

Laura admitted that her husband was abusive to her and their children, and had refused to go to therapy with her. "I try to pretend I'm happy a lot," Laura said tearfully. We told Laura that she needed to be honest about her feelings, and to stop pretending she was happy. By staying in the marriage, she was enabling her husband to continue doing the hurtful things he was doing, as though giving her tacit approval. Without actually telling her to leave the marriage, we encouraged her that by being on her own and making a life for herself, she would discover and tap inner strength that she didn't know she possessed. Terry said to her, "A bad relationship is never better than being alone. Besides, you aren't alone. You have your family, your children, your spirit guides around you, and you have our support too!" For Laura, step number one was to stop living a lie—trying to make a bad marriage work while putting her children in harm's way. Step number two was to recognize that she had options--healthy options--and much more power to create her life than she realized.

For over twenty years, as intutive success coaches, we have counseled people in every walk of life, from housewives to Fortune 500 executives, artists, doctors, lawyers, and even psychics! Because we have devoted our lives to our own physical, emotional and spiritual growth, we have developed the sixth sense to cut through the social "masks" that people present to the world. In a short time, we can address the most important issues of a person's life and what may be blocking that person's growth, abundance, health, and ability to manifest his or her dreams. When you tap into your own intuition and move powerfully into the next phase of your life, you will delight and amaze yourself, and will likely impress yourself when you take the time to do this.

Neuroscientist Candace Pert says, "It is a scientific fact that we can feel what others feel—emotional resonance. The oneness of all life is based on this simple reality. Our molecules of emotion are all vibrating together." If we truly believe that we are all one entity, one living breathing force in the Universe, and we can feel the feelings of others, why stop there? Why not know the thoughts of others? Why not believe that we can hear the subtle voices of the cosmos?

Why not decide that we can know the unknowable...the past, the future?

Printed in the United States
138743LV00001B/130/A